Fruitflesh

Fruitflesh

Seeds of Inspiration for
Women Who Write

GAYLE BRANDEIS

HarperSanFrancisco
A Division of HarperCollins*Publishers*

HarperCollins books may be purchased for educational, business, or sales promotional use. For information please write: Special Markets Department, HarperCollins Publishers Inc., 10 East 53rd Street, New York, NY 10022.

HarperCollins Web site: http://www.harpercollins.com
HarperCollins®, 📖®, and HarperSanFrancisco™ are trademarks of HarperCollins Publishers Inc.

FIRST HARPERCOLLINS PAPERBACK EDITION PUBLISHED IN 2004

Library of Congress Cataloging-in-Publication Data
Brandeis, Gayle.
Fruitflesh: seeds of inspiration for women who write / Gayle Brandeis.
p. cm.
ISBN 0–06–058718–0 (paperback)
1. Authorship. I. Title.
PN147.B69   2001
808'.02'082—dc21   2001039685

04 05 06 07 08 ❖ RRD(H) 10 9 8 7 6 5 4 3 2 1

For my parents, who gave me this body
For my children, who came through this body
For my husband, who makes me grateful
to live in this body every day

Write your self, your body must be heard.

HÉLÈNE CIXOUS

If a woman wants to be a poet,
she must dwell in the house of the tomato.

ERICA JONG

Contents

FOUR **Branches**

PART ONE

Seeds

*The impetuous seed of creation does not exactly
come forth on little cat feet.*

GEORGIANNE COWAN,
from "The Sacred Womb"

Preface

Where otherwise words were, flow discoveries,
freed all surprised out of the fruit's flesh.
RAINER MARIA RILKE

A strawberry changed my life.

It was my senior year of high school. At the time, I lived in, lived for, the heady world of ideals. Truth. Justice. Beauty. Spirit. Capital-I Ideals, which seemed—blessedly, I thought—to transcend the body. I was not very comfortable in my own skin as a teenager and found the body altogether too messy, too unpredictable, too fraught with humiliation and pain for my taste. I strove for something "higher" than what I perceived to be the illusion of the senses, the crudeness of physicality. Books were my escape, writing my refuge. At the time, I believed language was removed from the body; words, to me, were pure spirit, pure, crystalline thought. I lived in a thin, rarefied air. I cut myself off from all sensations below my chin. I cut myself off from the world around me.

Then a strawberry woke me up.

My favorite class at the time was philosophy. The teacher, Ms. Sweers, came into the classroom that day and dropped a crate of berries onto her desk. The fruit quivered lush and red inside the box. A sweet, loamy fragrance filled the air. Despite my mind's attempt to stay on top of my salivary glands, my mouth began to water.

Ms. Sweers walked around the classroom and placed a berry on each student's desk. The fruit glowed in front of us like little lanterns.

"Don't start eating yet," Ms. Sweers cautioned, to the frustrated moans of the class.

She sat back down at her desk and put a single berry on her palm.

"I want you each to fully experience your berry," she said. "Take five minutes to explore it with all of your senses but taste. Look at it closely. Breathe in its smell. Notice every texture, every nook and cranny. Give this berry the respect, the attention, it deserves. You may begin."

I picked up my strawberry, not expecting much. I had eaten countless berries in my life, after all. What was so special about this one? I loved Ms. Sweers, though, and was willing to go along with whatever she had in mind. I was sure there was some lesson to follow, some esoteric wisdom to be imparted after the frivolous exercise. I didn't realize the strawberry itself, the experience itself, would become the teacher.

Quickly, I discovered that I had never really looked at a strawberry before, not up close. As I carefully examined the nubbin of fruit, I wondered if I had ever looked, truly looked, at anything before. The scales, as they say, began to fall from my eyes. Everything seemed magnified. The strawberry became infinitely fascinating—its satiny skin, its intricate pattern of seed, its shaggy crown of delicately veined leaves. Was the whole world this richly complex? How much else had escaped my attention? I lifted the berry to my nose and breathed the scent deep into my lungs. My fingertips tingled against the edges of the leaves, thrilled with each curve of berry flesh. My senses emerged from their coma and sang.

I was startled by the intensity of my response to the fruit. When the five minutes were up and it was time to eat, I felt torn. I didn't want to put the berry in my mouth—I didn't want to say good-bye to its precious, singular body. At the same time, I wanted the berry inside me. I wanted to merge with it, draw it deep into my cells. I wanted to feel it coursing through my blood.

Ms. Sweers told us to take another five minutes to eat the fruit. Eat with mindfulness, she told us. Be aware of every texture against your lips, your tongue, the roof of your mouth. Be aware of each nuance of taste, each shadow of sour and sweet.

I rolled part of the berry around on my tongue. The sensations inside my mouth were so exquisite they almost hurt. As bits of fruit slid luxuriantly down my throat, I knew I had never felt so alive before in my life.

After those five minutes were up, Ms. Sweers asked us to write a haiku about our time with the strawberry. I wasn't sure I could do it. How could I distill such a monumental experience into a mere seventeen syllables? How could I capture the voluptuousness of the moment with such slender letters? My whole body hummed, as if the berry had filled me with its own vibrant red energy. I picked up my pen.

I don't remember the entire haiku I wrote that day, only the last line: *A small heart beats in my mouth*. When it was my turn to read my poem out loud, some of the kids in the class said, "Ewwww," but I didn't mean anything gross by those words. I just wanted to acknowledge the berry's aliveness. I wanted to acknowledge the way it brought me to life.

My writing changed irrevocably that day. Most of my high school poetry until then had been impassioned but unembodied rants against consumerism and the vague injustices of society. After the strawberry, my writing became much more lush, more connected to the environment, to my body.

I discovered that the capital-I Ideals I loved to write about were all the more palpable when I rooted them in the real world. "Love is the meaning of life" is a nice sentiment, but I began to realize it wouldn't hit home the way an image of a woman lifting a wedge of orange to her dying husband's mouth would.

I also discovered I didn't always have to write about the "big" issues to give my work power. I began to see it as my task to bear witness to the moment, to give voice to the incredible world around and inside me. I knew that if I could learn to pay deep attention to life, the way I had with the strawberry, I could begin to heal my relationship with my own flesh, my own creativity. I could tap into the pain and shame of my body and release it with words. I could explore my senses, my pleasures, and release them, too— both in my body and on the page. When I wrote about the fuzzy, feverish feeling on the first day of my period or the way the light spilled across the kitchen table, I could let the world speak, in all its wonderful, terrible beauty, through my fingertips, my tongue.

My experience of my body, of myself as a woman, forever changed that day in philosophy class. As I swallowed the plush fruit, I began to sense the fruitfulness, the sweet wildness, that lived inside my own skin. I began to want to unleash it.

That strawberry launched me on my life's path. It has been my quest ever since to unite body and word, language and flesh. In the process, I discovered I wanted to help other women writers tap into the vast, luscious creativity that simmers inside all our bodies. *Fruitflesh* is born of that desire. The pages are still dripping with strawberry juice.

Introduction

Call it a fruit. Call it the body's language,
Renascent itch that says I am alive.

RACHEL HADAS, from "Pomegranate Variations"

Our bodies are fruit. Our bodies are luscious, ripe, full of slick seeds.

Our bodies are fruitful. We can bring forth life from our deepest center. We can spray elaborate fountains of milk. We can give birth to stories and poems and paintings and bread and bowls and whole new worlds of ideas. Our ovaries are twin passion fruits nestled inside our bellies, packed with luminous seeds of possibility. We are all brimming with creative juice.

The word *fruit* comes from the Latin *fructus*, which means "that which is used or enjoyed." Our bodies are ours to use and enjoy fully, down to the last sticky drop. I wrote *Fruitflesh* to help us as women and as writers learn to enjoy our bodies and gain access to our own organic creative power. Our whole history is written in our flesh. Every pleasure, every pain we've experienced is encoded in our cells. As writers, we have a limitless store of material swirling underneath our own skin. When we bring awareness to our bodies, we bring new life, our own life, into our writing. As we open our senses, our capacity for connection with the world outside and within us increases tremendously, and we open the way for some amazing writing to pour forth.

Unfortunately, in our media-saturated culture, we are taught to live our bodies from the outside. We are taught to be concerned only about how we look, about what numbers blink when we step on the scale, about what size skirt we can zip ourselves into. We diet, we starve, we binge, we purge, we smoosh ourselves into girdles and push-up bras, all because of some Madison Avenue– and Hollywood-created image that tells us how we "should" look. As women, we are not taught, at least not by the popular media, to respect the deep wisdom and pleasures of our bodies—no matter what age or shape or ethnicity we may be. As a result, we are often cut off from our bodies' authentic joys and stories, the creativity that pulses so powerfully within us. I want this book to help us break through the tough, artificial, culturally imposed rind and release the sweet, juicy, creative flesh that is our birthright.

I am deeply saddened by the fact that throughout history, women who have written of themselves as fruitflesh have been punished for it. Ho Xuan Huang, an eighteenth-century Vietnamese poet, was often arrested for writing poems such as this about her own creative body:

JACKFRUIT
I am like a jackfruit on the tree.
To taste you must plug me quick, while fresh,
The skin rough, the pulp thick, yes,
But oh, I warn you against touching—
The rich juice will gush and stain your hands.

In the twentieth century, Portuguese poet Maria Teresa Horta was imprisoned for her sexually frank poetry. One of her poems ends with these lines:

I am lost to time
I am lost to time

enclosed in my
fruit
with breath inside

Fruit with breath inside. That seems like such a perfect description of a woman's body to me—juicy, sweet, breathing flesh.

According to Barbara Walker in *The Woman's Dictionary of Symbols and Sacred Objects,* a popular symbol for Truth and Sincerity in old Europe was a peach with one leaf attached to the stem. This symbol represented the union of heart (the fruit) and tongue (the leaf).

This is what we should strive for when we write—a union of heart and tongue (and hand and belly and throat and all the rest of our body). When we write from our fruitflesh, our words will be imbued instantly with truth and sincerity. Fruitflesh is not simple flesh—it is intelligent flesh, spirited flesh. It is the *soma,* the place where body and mind and spirit have no division. Our bodies are the repository for all our experiences, all our emotions, all our truest stories. We can capture our own wholeness, our own integrity on the page, when we allow our fruitflesh to speak.

Turn your attention inside your skin for a moment. Are you sitting? Lying down? Where are your hands? How does your scalp feel right now? Your belly? How is your body responding to my words—do you feel any hesitation bunched in your shoulders, maybe some anticipation sizzling in your chest? Do you want to sigh?

I hold my pen, scratch it against the page. You hold this page before you. Our hands, our eyes, connect, be it indirectly. Writing is a physical act. Our fingertips are highly sensitive. We write to touch.

I hope this book will allow you, as a woman and a writer, to begin to acknowledge and gain access to your body's own fruitful, creative power. As we come to honor the deep wisdom of our bodies, we also come to honor one another—our connectedness as women, as well as the wonder of our diversity, our individual creative talents. We are a vast orchard of succulent fruits. We come in all colors and sizes and stages of ripeness. Our flavors may be different, but they are all equally delicious.

The exercises and meditations in this book are designed to wake up both your body and your writing. You can think of them as juicings, as they serve to tap into and release the language that flows inside your own fruitflesh. The book follows the growing season—each section marks a new stage in the evolution of a fruit tree, from seed to root to full ripeness and back to seed again—but you don't need to follow the page order to ensure your own growth. Let your instinct be your guide; you can easily pluck a leaf before you plumb your roots or after you explore the buds ready to blossom inside you. You may want to start a *Fruitflesh* journal to keep all your writings in one place, a juicy document of your own unfolding.

The exercises in the book can be adapted to any writing genre. If you are a fiction writer, you can apply the exercises to your characters to get to know them in a deeper way. If you are a poet, the exercises may jump-start a poem with a body-centered image or sensation. If you are a journal writer or essayist, the exercises will give you rich material for your work as well as provide tools for greater self-awareness. Slither in and out between genres throughout the book as you are moved to. You may want to write a character study here, a poem there, a personal essay somewhere else, a hybrid of forms later. Listen to your body, your "gut instinct," what you "feel in your bones," and trust whatever shape your writing decides to take.

In her book *Food and Healing*, Annemarie Colbin writes, "Fruits . . . help the body and spirit work harmoniously together. Fruit eating also supports artistic expression, which in a broad sense could be to a human as a blossom is to a plant." Let the earth's most creative flesh inspire you from the inside out.

I hope you'll have a chance to savor some real fruit while you read *Fruitflesh*. The lessons of the book will be that much more luscious if you are able to experience them with your senses as well as your mind. I am a big fan of hands-on, tongues-on learning. If you don't like a particular fruit, though, or if none is accessible while you read the fruitflesh meditations, you can always visualize (and oral-ize and tactile-ize and olfactory-ize) the exercises. But do try to sink your teeth in, at least once.

I extend to you a delicious welcome to this book and hope that, through it, your own fruitflesh will blossom and welcome its sweet self home.

PART TWO

Roots

These days

*whatever you have to say, leave
the roots on, let them
dangle*

And the dirt

*Just to make clear
where they come from*
CHARLES OLSON

Where do your words come from?

Delve deep into your roots—the roots that connect your body to your family, to the earth itself, the roots that dangle beneath your desire to write. Your words will blossom most freely when they are grounded in your own fertile soil.

Fruitflesh Meditation: Mango

Hold a mango in your hand. Notice how solid it feels, rooted firmly in its own skin. The flesh inside is incredibly sexy—moist and slick, saturated with shades of sunset and intense, ambrosial flavor. The mango is wild but centered, its seed supportive as a spine.

Slice off a wedge of mango. Bend the fruit back, like a neck arched in pleasure. Explore the sweet flesh with your tongue, your teeth. Devour the fruit until your whole face is slippery with its juice.

Let your writing be like this feast—bold, sensual, unapologetic. Enter into it fully, with your whole body, without hesitation.

The Cellar

The apples in the cellar
are black, and dying inside their skins.
They pray all night in their bins,
but nobody listens;
they will be neither food nor trees.
ANNIE DILLARD, from "Feast Days"

Step down into your body's own root cellar, the dark place where you store all your yet-untold stories. Perhaps it is tucked beneath your liver; perhaps it is under your heart. Shine a light into the corners. What can you see? Is there a musty box of potential poems you've been meaning to unpack for years but haven't found the "right time" quite yet? Is there a germ of a story sealed in plastic because you were too busy or too afraid to begin writing the real thing? Can you still hear the unwritten words singing under their packing materials, or have their voices been muffled by time?

Now is the time to do some unwrapping, some airing out. If we don't tell the stories that ask to come through us, they die inside their skins, under our own skin; they become neither food nor trees. Choose one of these stories, hold it close to your heart, and carry it back up into the light. Even if you write just one paragraph, just one line of the piece, you'll prevent it from rotting away. And who knows? It could blossom into something beautiful and nourishing. It could be the treasure you didn't realize you were carrying inside you all this time.

Organic Expression

The crude American palate . . . paralyzes all flavor,
stiffens the melon, anesthetizes the strawberry, and
changes a ring of pineapple into fiber more textile than
edible.

    The fruit room-temperature, the water in the glass
cold: that is how water and fruit seem best. What is one to
make of a fruit that is removed, like a cooling planet,
from the warmth that formed it? An apricot picked and
eaten in the sun is sublime.

COLETTE, from "Flora and Pomona"

Writing, too, is best when it is not removed from the warmth that formed it, when it remains close to its source.

Colette bemoans the "crude American palate" for taking all of the native, sensual flavor and texture away from fruit. When we tailor our own words for mass consumption, we, too, lose the delicious wildness that can be found only within pure, organic expression.

If you find your writing getting away from you, bring your focus back to the body. Reel your words back under your skin, to what you're experiencing in the moment—the taste of sourdough in your mouth, the way the light hits the blue lip of the water glass, the scent of dirty laundry wafting across the room. Let yourself be fully present, in the world and on the page. Tell the story only you can tell, the one that hums inside your cells, the one that only you can release. Let the warmth of your body bring your words to full ripeness.

Opening the Velvet Rope

This Way
*Slicing a peach
for her cereal, the poet
hears a rhythm, feels
anticipation the eager body
thinks is sex. Let it.
But keep the mind cool,
receptive, unresisting
as emptied houses the sea
takes when the break-
wall gives. Leave
the radio off, the phone
unhooked. Let newspapers bleach
on the front steps. Whatever
comes, pulsing
astonished on your desk, gawky,
unbeautiful, nothing
you want to claim except
the glint in its eye, that familial
wink, names it kin—let it.*
Sally Croft

When words want to come through us—gawky, unbeautiful words—how do we let them in without shaking our heads, clucking our tongues, saying, "Oh, no, you're not gorgeous enough to walk past this velvet rope. This club is exclusive. You don't belong here"? Our inner critics can be merciless; they want the words on the page to be sterilized to perfection. But who wants to shake it on a dance floor that's full of only impossibly manicured, airbrushed folk? The goofy drunken guests who make fools of themselves, the wild child dancers with twigs in their unbrushed hair make the party so much more interesting. How do we open up the velvet rope, make room for even the unwashed words, the unfashionable words, the words with warts and moles to sashay on through?

This is where the concept of timed freewriting comes in handy. Set a timer for ten or fifteen minutes, and write at least until the bell rings (if you feel moved to keep going afterward, by all means do!). The most important thing, as Natalie Goldberg reminds us, is to keep your hand moving. Don't let your judging, critical mind disrupt the flow. Let whatever wants to pour out, pour out unhindered. If you keep your fingers flying fast enough, your inner critic won't have a chance to cluck its tongue.

You can use this technique for any of the exercises in the book. If you feel like writing about breasts after reading the "Breast" chapter, for example, but don't know where to start, you can set your timer for ten minutes and write "Breasts, breasts, breasts" until the floodgates open. Who knows—you may start with breasts and end up writing about your second-grade teacher's elbow. That's fine. Let whatever wants to emerge, emerge, pulsing and astonished on the page. You can always groom it into respectability later, if the occasion calls for it.

Writing Rituals

The poet Schiller used to keep rotten apples under the lid of his desk and inhale their pungent bouquet when he needed to find the right word. Then he would close the drawer, although the fragrance remained in his head. Researchers at Yale University discovered that the smell of spiced apples has a powerful elevating effect on people and can even stave off panic attacks. Schiller may have sensed this all along. Something in the sweet, rancid mustiness of those apples jolted his brain into activity while steadying his nerves.

DIANE ACKERMAN, from *A Natural History of the Senses*

Writers often create rituals to help them enter the creative process.

Isabel Allende starts all of her books on January 8, the day she began her first novel. She surrounds herself with pictures of her loved ones as well as pictures related to what she plans to write about. She has the words of Pablo Neruda nearby, either in sight or under the computer, to represent her homeland, Chile. She sips mango tea. And she begins to write.

Are there certain things you always do before you write? Do you play a round of solitaire, like Maya Angelou, or put a certain album on the stereo, like Carolyn See? If you don't already have a ritual, try creating one. Eat three grapes, or chant a little invocation, or light a candle before you start to write. Dance or sing or take a whiff of vanilla or stand on your head. Whatever you think will help launch you into writing mode.

Creation Myths

A Peruvian legend tells how the guarana fruit came into being. A couple belonging to the Maues people wanted a child. They asked the king of the gods, Tupa, to give them a child so their happiness would be complete. Knowing they were good people with good hearts, Tupa brought a beautiful baby boy into their lives.

The boy grew to be compassionate, handsome, generous, and wise. Jurupari, the god of darkness, was extremely envious of the boy and the peace that surrounded him. One day, when the boy went to gather fruits in the forest, Jurupari turned himself into a serpent and bit the boy, delivering a fatal dose of venom.

As the parents dealt with their inconsolable grief, a thunderstorm rolled into the village. Lightning struck the ground near the mother. She realized it was a sign from Tupa, telling her to plant her child's eyes in the earth. A new plant would grow there, Tupa told her, bearing wonderful fruit.

The mother planted her son's eyes in the soil. In that spot grew the guarana. Under the bright red skin, a black seed with a white coating sat in the center of each fruit, like a human eye.

Do you know the tale of your own beginnings? If you know the true story of your conception, your birth, write about it. If you don't know, try to find out where and when you were created.

Now, whether or not you know the real facts, write about how you wish your life began. Spin an elaborate creation myth that tells how your body came to be alive in the world.

Grandmother Stories

No amount of knowledge can shake my grandma out of me;
or my Aunt Maud; or my mama, who didn't just bite an apple
with her big white teeth. She split it in two.
Ruth Stone, from "Pokeberries"

In what ways do you carry your mother inside your body? Your grandmother? Do their voices ever emerge in your writing? Do you sometimes startle yourself by using a turn of phrase—"the bee's knees," maybe—or a certain word that spent a lot of time in your mother's mouth? Do you ever feel that your voice is not just your own, that your throat, your pen serve as pipelines to earlier generations?

Take your body back to its roots. Enter the body of your mother or grandmother or great-grandmother. What would it be like to live inside her skin? How did she feel about her own body—as a child, a teenager, a young mother, an older woman? Write from her voice. Let your body tell the tale of the bodies that came before you, the bodies that brought you into being, the bodies that still sing through your blood.

Family Language

In the early 1900s, my great-aunt Mick went to get her portrait taken. At the time, women were expected to purse their mouths in a tiny ring in portraits, almost as if they were whistling. The photographer asked Mick to say "prunes" very daintily to give her mouth that "oooo" shape. Aunt Mick chose to say the word in Yiddish instead. *Prunes* in Yiddish is *flahmen*, which she drew out into an extended foghorn of a word—"Flahhhhhmen." Her portrait looks like she is saying "ahhh" at the doctor's office, her mouth wide open in a very unladylike way.

Do you know any language-related tales about your family? Were your ancestors' last names changed when they entered Ellis Island? Did any of them use words in radical, playful, hurtful ways?

How did members of your family use language when you were a child? Did your family choose words carefully, painstakingly, or was there always a frenetic verbal Ping-Pong match at the dinner table? Did you grow up with more than one language in the house? Were you surrounded by silence or din?

Write a scene of dialogue from your childhood. Who said what? What did you say? How did you say it? Was there anyone in your family with a real love for language? Try writing from that family member's voice.

Making Pilgrimage

and i taste the
seasons of my birth. mangoes. papayas.
drink my woman/coconut milks
stalk the ancient grandfathers
sipping on proud afternoons
walk like a song round my waist
tremble like a new/born/child troubled
with new breaths
and my singing
becomes the only sound of a
blue/black/magical/woman. walking.
womb ripe. walking. loud with mornings. walking.
making pilgrimage to herself. walking.

Sonia Sanchez, from "Present"

What is your ancestral land? What fruits did your ancestors eat? Plantains in Africa? Lychees in China? Chokecherries in North America? Grapes in Italy? Apples in England? Papayas in Mexico? Rambutan in Indonesia?

When you make pilgrimage to your homeland(s), either literally or figuratively on the page, you make pilgrimage to yourself. How does your body reflect the soil that still circles through you?

In her seminar at Antioch University, "Interior Journeys: Remembering the Land," Tia Oros, a woman of Zuni heritage, asked students to write from the voice of their ancestral homelands. How would your own home soil speak? What would it want to tell you? Let it speak to you, through you, on the page. Let it use its own rich, fruited tongue.

Earth

A poet in a world without onions,
in a world without apples,
regards the earth as a great fruit.
ERICA JONG, from "Fruits and Vegetables"

Even in a world with apples and onions, the earth is a great fruit. We ourselves are fruits of the earth, rooted to it as surely as any fruit tree. Our writing can benefit from this rich connection.

Before Cheyenne storytellers launched into their tales, they smoothed the earth before them, then marked the soil and touched some dirt to their bodies. They did this to give the Creator witness, to acknowledge that the Creator made humans and the earth, but it also gave the earth witness. By physically touching the earth, the storyteller grounded himself, reminded himself of his connection to the soil. Touching the earth, he touched the source of his tales.

Alice Walker found the earth to be a source of comfort as she wrote *Possessing the Secret of Joy*. The book, centered on the practice of genital mutilation, was born out of deep anger and sadness. In an interview she said, "By the time I actually started writing the book, I was in such a state of grief that the only thing that sustained me was going outside and lying face down on the earth. Somehow I got the energy that I always get from the earth directly."

What can you do to connect your writing with the earth, to connect yourself with the earth when writing gets intense? Touch your forehead with dirt like the Cheyenne storyteller, lie down on the earth like Alice Walker, or find your own way to ground yourself and your writing.

Landscape

what did it mean to leave behind that body aroused by
the feel of hot wind, ecstatic with the smell of sage, so
excited i could barely contain myself as we left pines
and high-blue eagle sky, and broke into the arid insect
country of the Okanagan with its jumping butterflies,
its smell, familiar as apricots, our mouths full of sweet
pulp, bare legs sticky with it, hot and itchy against
each other, against the pelt of the dog, his rank dog-day
smell as we rode the turns of the road down into summer,
real summer on our skin—do you remember? how could
you not?

DAPHNE MARLATT, from "Ana Historic"

Remember a landscape. A mountain range that continues to saturate your senses. A meadow that breathes against your skin, that speaks to you in wind and leaf and birdsong.

When poet Pattiann Rogers moved from Missouri to Texas, she missed her home state desperately. She closed her eyes and conjured up fall in Missouri, her favorite season, the best she could, remembering and naming every little detail, from "the rocky earth, sometimes orange with iron" to "the taste of October." She writes, "During those moments I realized for the first time that I loved a landscape, loved it like my own body, that it *was* my own body, my body and my pattern of perception, that it had informed and constructed me."

What landscape has informed and constructed you? What corner of the earth have you felt a deep union with? Bring this place—and your body's response to it—to full, three-dimensional life on the page. Remember and name each little detail, from the wild mustard scent of the breeze to the burrs that clung to your socks long after you ran through the scrubby field.

Our Native Fields

*Most of us are still related to our native fields as the
navigator to undiscovered islands in the sea. We can any
afternoon discover a new fruit there which will surprise
us by its beauty or sweetness. So long as I saw in my
walks one or two berries whose names I did not know, the
proportion of the unknown seemed indefinitely, if not
infinitely, great.*

HENRY DAVID THOREAU

So often we forget to see what is right in front of our eyes.
We often don't take the time to pay close attention to the very spe-
cific place on earth where we live. We forget how much mystery
surrounds us.

I once met a man at a party whose father, in retirement, had
taken a job as a sidewalk inspector. His assignment was to walk
around and look at sidewalks all day, noting cracks, litter, any
changes that could affect the cement paths in some way. I thought,
what a wonderful job! A job like that would really force you to pay
attention to the particulars of your environment, to notice all the
grades of cement and stone, to recognize certain footprints and
wheel marks, to see all the little plants growing in the cracks, the
bugs that skitter across.

Go for a walk in your neighborhood. Keep your senses open.
Try to notice things you've never noticed before—a chalky, sharp-
smelling berry . . . a red-eyed insect with transparent green wings
. . . the way the paint is chipped on a certain fence post. What do
you discover? What stories might these discoveries tell?

Home

... *Poetry roots itself in the dreamer*
slowly, it can be sickness or health but settles
into the soil of ancestors, carried over who knows what seas
in the mouth of an extinct bird, on an insect's
back. Slowly the leaves unfold, slowly you learn
to read them, learn to risk the lightning cage,
the shower, the smash of edible and inedible
fruit, to open your arms to a closed gate with a plaque
that asks you if you know when you're at home.
JUDY MICHAELS, from "On the Sour Sop Tree
in Elizabeth Bishop's Yard, Key West"

How do you know when you're home? For some people *home*
can be pinned down to a specific address; for others, it's a feeling
that can't be rooted to any particular location. Our bodies often tell
us when we are home—a sense of contentment between the ribs, a
profound, cellular sense that we are right where we belong.

Write about home. Rooms you've lived in ... apartments,
houses, neighborhoods, cities, states, countries. People who feel
like home; pets, books, articles of clothing. Food that tastes like
home, smells that take you there. Familiar flora, fauna, weather.
Body as home, as the place where you most truly *live*. Ask yourself,
is it possible to be fully at home anywhere if you're not at home
inside your own flesh?

Think about the vocabulary of home as you write. Is your
home a hut, a dwelling, a castle, a "space," a state of being? What
words connote home to you—*brick* or *pillow? Wood* or *welcome? Skin*
or *sigh?*

Body Commandments

Keep your legs crossed, Mother said. Drinking
leads to babies. Don't hang around street corners.
I rushed to gulp moonshine on corners, hip outthrust.
So why in the butter of my brain does one marble tablet
shine bearing my mother's commandment, eat fruit?
MARGE PIERCY, from "Eat Fruit"

What commandments did your parents give you about your body as you were growing up? Do they still shine in your brain like marble tablets, affecting the way you live in your body now?

Write a list, in commandment form, of the body rules you grew up with—"Thou shalt not touch thyself," "Thou shalt only eat 1200 calories a day," "Thou shalt not lose thy virginity with a tampon." If any of these commandments have harmed your relationship with your body, feel free to lift the tablets over your head and hurl them against the ground. Write a response to each commandment. You can list all the ways in which you've broken it, all the ways you've lived under its shadow. If you were lucky enough to grow up in a house with positive body lessons—"Thou shalt listen to thy gut," "Thou shalt practice safe sex"—write a response to those as well.

Now write a new list of body commandments for yourself. Make sure they are nurturing commandments, commandments that will give your body pleasure and peace—"Thou shalt get a massage at least every other month," "Thou shalt savor each bite of strawberry." Share this list with your friends, your daughters— and encourage them to write their own!

Religion and the Body

Mary is offering the Baby Jesus an apple.
At least it looks like an apple
from where we stand. But it could easily be
her breast, the blush of the full nipple
cupped in her hand like a pip, held
toward his parted mouth. Or it could be a ripe
bonbon of manna, a heavenly food, or the earth,
juicy, buzzing, spice-popping globe.

PATTIANN ROGERS, from "Still Life Abroad"

Some people may find this poem by Pattiann Rogers pro-
fane, offensive, in the way it celebrates, sensualizes, the body of the
Virgin Mother. The warmth of Mary's chaste flesh, "the blush of
the full nipple," is rarely acknowledged, even though it pulsed
beneath her cool blue and white robes.

In much Western spirituality, there is a huge rift between
body and spirit. Women who grow up under dogma that teaches
that the body is impure, base, often have trouble enjoying their
"sinful" physicality. Organized religion can sometimes seem at odds
with the body, with the idea that spirit breathes fully within the
flesh. At the same time, many religious rituals are lush, full of sen-
sory pleasures, such as the etrog fruit shaken in all directions during
the Jewish holiday of Sukkot or the incense burned at Catholic
mass.

How did your religious upbringing, or lack of it, teach you to
relate to your body? Do you still feel the effects of those teachings
in how you relate to your body, how you write about your body,
even today?

Some writers find that rhythms from their religious upbring-
ing are so deeply ingrained in them that their work echoes those
rhythms. Sharon Olds has said that the first four lines of her poems
often follow the "Episcopalian quatrain" of the hymns she grew up

singing. Marge Piercy roots many of her poems in the cadence of Hebrew prayer.

What are some of the rituals of your spiritual upbringing? How was your body involved? Think about rising and sitting in temple or church, lighting candles, meditating in zazen, kneeling and receiving the body and blood of Christ into your mouth. Write about the movements, the rhythms, the sensory impressions you remember from your childhood sabbaths and holidays.

The Seder Orange

Baruch Atoh adonai, Elohainu Melech HaOlam shehecheyonu v'kiymonu v'higi-onu lazman hazeh.

Thank you, Source of all Blessing, kind Creator, for keeping us alive and sustaining us and allowing us to reach this time.
Traditional *bracha*, or Hebrew blessing, sung when eating a fruit for the first time that season

For the past few decades, many Jewish women have chosen to place an orange on the seder table at Passover. The citrus glows like a ripe sun next to the bitter herbs, the roasted egg, all the other traditional seder foods. When the fruit is sectioned and shared at the feast, people fill their mouths with a juicy affirmation of female power.

There are many stories about the origin of this ritual. Some believe it started when an elderly Jewish man made a comment that having a woman as a rabbi made as much sense as putting an orange on a seder table; others believe this comment was directed at lesbian rabbis in particular. One telling of the story has the man saying that a woman rabbi makes as much sense as a crust of bread (a forbidden food during Passover) on the seder plate. A woman, so the story goes, replied that a female rabbi is more like an orange on the seder plate than a crust of bread—she represents a transformation of tradition, not a transgression. Whatever the true root of the ritual may be, placing an orange upon the seder table has become an act of defiance for women, an act of reclamation and celebration. It's an act that says *we belong here*. We bring so much richness to the table.

Ritual can be a profound tool for women who want to break through perceived limitations and claim (or reclaim) our own power. We can turn a wall into a window, sometimes with the simplest act.

Have you been told there are certain things you can't do or say or write about because you are a woman, because "nice girls" wouldn't explore such things, whether sex or pain or any other topic that reaches deep into the body's experience and memory? How have those limitations on your creative life become so ingrained in your own body and mind that you have constricted your own scope of expression? You may want to keep an orange on your writing table (or create another ritual) to remind yourself that you are welcome here—in your body, on the page—and that you are free to experience yourself, express yourself fully.

Expanding Horizons

One day, I was throwing stones at a guava tree, trying to knock down a ripe guava, when the Red Girl came along and said, "Which one do you want?" After I pointed it out, she climbed up the tree, picked the one I wanted off its branch, climbed down, and presented it to me. How my eyes did widen and my mouth form an "o" at this. I had never seen a girl do this before. All the boys climbed trees for the fruit they wanted, and all the girls threw stones to

knock the fruit off the trees. But look at the way she
climbed that tree: better than any boy.
JAMAICA KINCAID, from *Annie John*

People sometimes come into our lives and expand our horizons by their example alone. Who has made eyes widen, who has made your mouth form an "o"? Who helped you see beyond your own self-imposed (or culturally imposed) limitations and made you realize the world was more full of possibility than you ever could have imagined? A teacher, maybe? A particularly courageous friend? An Olympic athlete? Your favorite writer? Write about this person and the walls he or she knocked down for you. How did it feel to suddenly be faced with so much new open space?

The People You Have

Big heart,
wide as a watermelon,
but wise as birth,
there is so much abundance
in the people I have
ANNE SEXTON, from "The Big Heart"

Writing is a solitary art. Hopefully, we can enter this solitude with the knowledge that there are people who love and support us as we venture into our own root cellars, our own rich mining shafts, people who will be there when we emerge, dusted with coal.

Sometimes, though, even when the love is abundant, our loved ones don't understand our desire to write. They may feel jealous of the time we spend at our computer or threatened by the new creative freedom we have found. Don't let this hinder your writing.

Your friends and family may yet come to realize that when you do what fulfills you, you're much better company! A frustrated writer is not much fun to be around. If your loved ones still don't understand, you can craft a letter that explains why you need to write, and you can knock their socks off with your fabulous talent in the process! Writing such a letter to yourself is a good idea, anyway; it can clarify what fuels your creative impulse, taking you straight to the heart, the roots, of what you want and need to express.

Needs

They wouldn't need much, would they? A few small fish,
an arrangement of figs. A little paper. A handful of
words.
CAROLE MASO, from *The American Woman in the Chinese Hat*

Think about what you need to be able to fit writing into your life, whether it's time or space or quiet. Is there anything you can pare away in order to devote more time to your art? Can you let the laundry pile up, cancel your cable subscription, keep the phone off the hook for an hour, let a friend take your kids one afternoon a week? Can you find a "room of your own" or even a small space—a park bench, a pillow—that you can allocate exclusively for your writing? If you are able to devote only ten minutes a day to the page, it will still help satisfy your essential creative needs. Guard those ten minutes with your life; they are sacred.

It's important to remember that one of the most important words in any writer's, and any woman's, vocabulary is *no*. When we learn to say no, without guilt, to those things that keep us from our desire, it creates more space for the things that make us say yes.

Fruitflesh Meditation: Ugli Fruit

The Ugli fruit is the only fruit with a trademarked name. The citrus fruit hails from Jamaica, but the name hails from Canada, where there was a great demand for more of that "ugly fruit" from the islands. Despite its name, the Ugli is not hideous. Its peel is simply less uniformly colored and textured than that of most citrus fruits. It is the size of a grapefruit, mottled on the outside with greens, oranges, and yellows. The pachydermic skin is thick and loose, easy to peel; the flesh inside is juicy, with a sweet, pungent tang.

Hold an Ugli fruit. Feel how it wears its name loosely, the fruit moving freely beneath the puffy skin. Peel the skin off. Hold the naked fruit in your hand. Feel its wholeness, the dignity it carries beneath its demeaning name. Gently remove a section and bite into the pulp. Taste its true beauty.

How have you been trademarked, labeled? How have those labels—"good girl," "bad girl," and the like—affected you and your work? Have you let yourself embody the labels, the trademarks other people have imposed upon you? Break free of those labels. They are not you. Leave them behind you like a pile of citrus peel. Feel the integrity of your own fruitflesh that pulses underneath. Let yourself blossom into your own rightful name.

PART THREE

Trunk

*This year I have planted my feet
on this ground*

*and am practicing
growing out of my legs
like a tree.*

LINDA LANCIONE MOYER,
from "Listen"

Our bodies are like tree trunks, simultaneously anchored in the earth and reaching toward the sun. Creativity surges inside us, green and alive; when we tune into our bodies, we can tap the force, the source, that brims in all our cells.

Fruitflesh Meditation: Kiwifruit

A kiwifruit is like a fuzzy brown egg, rather dull and unassuming on the outside. When you cut one open, though, a bold and glistening emerald fruit greets you.

Take a tentative bite of the kiwi skin. It tastes like cardboard and may even make your tongue itch. Bite further, past the skin, into the heart of the fruit. Let its sweet deep color fill your mouth.

When you write, your words may feel fuzzy and brown and dull at first. Don't let that dissuade you. Treasure is often buried under unassuming ground. Keep writing. Keep going deeper. Eventually you will hit the vibrant green fruitheart of words.

Belly

Just as a peach or plum or apricot holds its seed, its creative source, deep in its center, so do we hold our creative energy in the center of our bodies. Life begins in the belly, as any mother knows. Movement begins in the belly, too; a dancer's "center" is found between the belly button and the pubic bone. If a dancer is disconnected from her center, she'll be off balance, out of whack. In martial arts and Eastern medicine traditions, the belly is considered the *hara* or *tan t'ien*, the center of energy and power. Our words spring from this source as well.

Can you feel your own "center"? Stand up, feet shoulder width apart. Keep your knees soft and slightly bent. Rock your hips back and forth awhile; then swing them side to side. Now move your hips in several big circles, first in one direction and then the other. Return to standing still. Can you feel an aliveness in your belly, a warmth? That is where your movement, your creative energy, springs from. If you still feel disconnected, take both of your hands and place them on your belly, below your navel. Rub them in a few circles vigorously in one direction, then in the other, to activate some aliveness in your center. As you do this, feel the words come to life in your body, churning, building up steam, ready to write their way into the world.

Tuning In

. . . What sap
went through that little thread
to make the cherry red!
Marianne Moore, from "Nevertheless"

Our bellies are our centers, but creative energy moves throughout our bodies like a sweet sap. It can gather and pulse in an ankle, the small of the back, a left earlobe, any part of our fruit-flesh.

We can tune in to our bodies to sense where, in the present moment, our creativity hums most loudly. This exercise is adapted from one used by Terry Wolverton in her yoga and writing workshops. You can practice it daily, as a creative check-in before you write, or any time you need to locate the creativity inside your skin.

Lie down on your back and close your eyes. Let your breath soften, deepen. Breathe relaxation into each part of your body, starting with your toes, flowing all the way up to your throat, your face. When you feel quiet, open, bring your awareness to the inside of your body. Explore your inner regions, the space inside your skin. Can you feel where your creativity pulses right now? Is it located in your vulva, your rib cage, the arch of your foot? What shape does it take? Does it have a color, a sound, a density?

Stay present with your creativity when you find it. See if it changes form, if it moves from one part of your body to another. Does it have its own voice? What might it want to say to you? Listen carefully; the wisdom that rises from the body is often stunning. When you are ready, write about your encounter.

Fruit with Breath Inside

We are fruit with breath inside, as Maria Teresa Horta writes. Breath is life. Breath invigorates us, fills our blood with oxygen, fills our bodies with vitality, fills our language with possibility. Breath, literally, "inspires" us.

Too often, as women, we walk around sucking our stomachs in, holding our breath. This is a sad commentary on how our society expects us to look, but the consequences run even deeper. Withholding breath withholds circulation, not to mention sensation. When we try to look like our stomachs are flatter than they are, we also flatten the sensation we could be experiencing in the lower half of our bodies. We disconnect ourselves from our creative center.

Suck in your tummy as tight as you can. Try writing about how this feels without exhaling or letting go of your muscles. It's not so easy, is it?

Now let your stomach be soft, whole, relaxed to its natural self. Let your breath be full, natural. Take the world and all its inspiration deep into your lungs. Exhale; give yourself back fully to your environment. Feel yourself as fruit filled with breath, filled with vital, vibrant, aliveness. Now write about your belly, how it feels when you don't constrict its movement. Let your breath imbue your words with its supple, subtle flow.

Voice

Voice a refusal of death. She heard it
and felt the atoms of her body shimmer,

along with all the struck, shimmering atoms
of the air. Voice like pomelo, mango,

jackfruit, papaya, voice like slow ripening,
gold juice, orange meat. Voice changeful as water.

Milagros knows it is her own voice, the one
she never used.

MARISA DE LOS SANTOS, from "Milagros Mourns the Queen of Scat"

How would you describe your own voice—on the page and off? Is your writing voice an extension of your speaking voice, or do they come from two different throats entirely? Does your voice ever feel walled in, packed into boxes—voice boxes—that you can't seem to open? What would it sound like if you finally set it free?

A good way to loosen up your vocal cords is to play with sound. Let yourself hum, growl, speak in many octaves of gibberish. Take a deep breath, and let big, deep sounds come up from your belly. See how high your voice is willing to go, how low you can let it fall; see how fast you can sing your favorite song, how slowly you can stretch it out. Limbering up our physical voice often frees our writing voice as well. Our voices are our instruments, especially if we plan to share our work at readings or small gatherings.

It is good practice for us as writers to also be aware of other people's voices, to listen deeply when people speak. How else can we capture the real rhythms of dialogue on the page?

Pay attention to people's voices, their varying cadences and musicality. Think of someone you speak with often. Try to describe his or her voice. Is it raspy? Nasal? Smooth and sweet as mango juice?

Keep your ears and mind and heart open, and your writing will speak in your clearest, truest voice.

Anatomy Lessons

Within the red serenity of each apple
in the bowl, a seething fortune of molecules
is expanding, uniting, transfiguring.
And at the epicenter of the onion's circle
of steady waves, even in that dark funnel,
there is a hard rush, a gathering
and differentiation of cells rudely forcing
upward toward light a sharp flume of green.
Beneath the quiet surface skin of the bulging
plum, many million microscopic teeth tear,
rip—pulp, fermentation. Tangled in the noiseless
core of one fragrant peach, twist and rear
many fearsome beasts, many fires.
PATTIANN ROGERS, from "Still Life Abroad"

So much happens under our skin. There is no still life in real life. At the molecular level, we are all in constant motion.

One summer I decided to take a survey course in anatomy and physiology. I was beginning serious inquiry into connecting writing with dance, writing with the body, and I thought I should gain a better understanding of what I was working with. The course was offered at the local community college as part of the nursing program. I was the only nonnursing student in the class, the only student who didn't have to be there.

That class was a constant revelation for me. We'd learn about cellular respiration, and I'd turn to the woman next to me and say, "Wow! Isn't that amazing!" As we sat in that classroom, our vitreous humors were refracting light waves, our tympanic membranes were vibrating, and thousands of synapses were crackling through our neurons. It wasn't just happening in the textbook. It was happening in us, would keep happening in us our entire lives.

Our bodies do so many things at once; their simultaneous processes are awe inspiring, humbling, absolutely miraculous. Our bodies are not solid. They are not like stones or pieces of wood. Bodies are not nouns; they are verbs. Bodies are rhythmic, pulsing, breathing organisms, and it follows that the writing that comes from an authentic experience of the body should be equally as musical, as dynamic.

Find an anatomy book. Discover what's going on inside your skin. How can you not be creative when all that marvelous activity is churning inside of you?

Write a love poem to your (or your lover's) kidneys, spine, hair follicles—any intricate, delicate part of the body that normally doesn't receive any attention. Give thanks to your synovial fluid! Wax rhapsodic over your mitochondria! All these parts are working together to create your own fruitflesh. They deserve the utmost appreciation, the deepest respect.

Skin Color

A crayon box is full of delicious colors—*plum, wild strawberry, vivid tangerine*. Fortunately, there is no longer a crayon called "flesh"; the crayon manufacturers have finally acknowledged that not everyone's complexion is apricot or peach. We come in so many luscious, complex shades.

How would you name your own skin tone? Avoid labels, stereotypes, that have already been applied to it. Give yourself a name that is not yet in any crayon box, a name that carries your own distinct luster.

Our epidermis is our largest organ; explore its different textures, its subtle, supple nuances. Does your color change throughout the year? How does it respond to heat, to sun, to cold, to touch?

Does the flesh stretched behind your ear differ at all from the span that curves behind your knee?

Imagine your skin as fruit; note if it's downy as a peach in some places, stippled as orange peel in others. Do you have slick persimmon surfaces, rough pineapple patches? Let the blank skin of the page reflect the shade and grain of your own succulent skin.

Identifying Marks

It is rare that the summer lets an apple go without streaking or spotting it on some part of its sphere. It will have some red stains, commemorating the mornings and evenings it has witnessed; some dark and rusty blotches, in memory of the clouds and foggy, mildewy days that have passed over it; and a spacious field of green reflecting the general face of Nature—green even as the fields; or a yellow ground, which implies a milder flavor—yellow as the harvest or russet as the hills.
Henry David Thoreau

Life leaves its mark on us. Every scar that puckers on our skin, every stretch mark, every wrinkle, every freckle tells a story of who we are and where we've been.

Tell some of these stories. Choose a scar, and explain how it came to decorate your body. Look at your freckles; do any of them create patterns together? Name the constellations they form across your body. Do the wrinkles of your knuckles crinkle into faces or swirl like knots on a tree? Do stretch marks streak like lightning across your hips? What growth brought them there? Has laughter carved little commas into your cheeks? Lay bare your "identifying marks," your unique physical identity, on the page.

Shedding Skins

PAJAMAS

My daughter's pajamas lie on the floor
inside out, thin and wrinkled as
peeled skins of peaches when you ease the
whole skin off at once.
You can see where her waist emerged, and her legs,
her arms, and head, the fine material
gathered in rumples like skin the caterpillar
ramped out of and left to shrivel.
You can see, there at the center of the bottoms,
the raised cotton seam like the line
down the center of fruit, where the skin first splits
and curls back. You can almost see the hard
halves of her young buttocks, the precise
stem-mark of her sex. Her shed
skin shines at my feet, and in the air there is a
sharp fragrance like peach brandy—
the birth-room pungence of her released life.
SHARON OLDS

How many different skins have you shed? How many bodies
have you lived inside?

Write about yourself, your body, from the time you were
newborn, three months old, three years old, seven, eleven, sixteen,
twenty-five, sixty—whichever years you wish to explore. You may
use photos to help jog your memory, but try to tap into cellular
memory, too. What were your hands like at five, at thirteen, at
thirty? How have your knees changed? Your feet? Your hair? What
shifts have taken place on your face? Have some characteristics
stayed remarkably the same over the years?

Try to remember what it really felt like to live inside your
skin at different ages, not just how you looked. If you are writing

fiction, you may want to delve into the evolving bodies of your characters as well.

To fully connect with the skin you live in now, you may want to blindfold yourself and touch your elbow, your heel, your hip, your breast. Taking the visual element out of the equation often helps us *feel* things with more openness and clarity. Write about what your fingertips discover.

Hands

Buddha's hand, or fingered citron, is a variety of citrus with several finger-thick projections reaching out from one end of the fruit. The fingers have no pulp inside; they are fruitskin all the way through. The peel can be eaten if candied, but the fruit is generally used for its fragrance. When set out in a room, it can sweeten the air for over a month. It is also often placed before Golden Buddhas as an offering, to ensure good luck and health. It holds a lot of magic in its citrusy hand. Our own hands are equally full of magic.

Take the time to look closely at your hands. Think of all the amazing things they do—the pleasure they give, the doors they open. Do you see any traces of your writing there? Do you have a "writer's bump" on the middle finger of your writing hand? Are you developing carpal tunnel in your wrists from hours of typing? Let your hands give each other a little massage. Soothe them with rich lotions. Give them both a kiss. Buy an ergonomic keyboard or a wrist rest to protect your precious appendages. Our hands help midwife our work into the world. They deserve our most lavish praise.

Whether we use a fountain pen or compose directly on a keyboard, our hands are intimately involved. Try switching to a different tool, if only to write a few notes or a journal entry. Use a keyboard if you normally use a pencil, a felt tip if you usually use a word processor. How does it feel different? Do the words come out at a different pace? Let your body find its own connection with the page as it uses the less familiar writing implement.

Be aware of how you write. Does your pen attack the paper? Do you tickle your typewriter keys? Do you caress the page with ink? If you kill your keyboard, try loving it. If your pencil barely skims the page, try pushing some passion into the graphite. How does the quality of writing change when the physical act of writing changes?

Emily Dickinson's Foot

The body is the great leveler. We all can share in the simple pleasure of tasting a plum, a strawberry, a spear of papaya, regardless of our age, our ethnicity, our size, our social status. We all have lips and tongues and salivary glands and stomachs. On the level of flesh, we find communal, poignant bond.

It is good to remember this when we are dazzled, intimidated, by someone else's writing.

It's easy to see writers we admire as being somehow godly, superhuman, something we could never become. It's easy for us to think of ourselves as lesser beings. It helps to remember that all writers write in their bodies. All writers have lungs and wrists and anuses. This awareness doesn't diminish the greatness of the writers we love; it makes them more human. Plus, it increases our own capacity for compassion and connection. It allows us to trust the creativity of our own bodies.

In an interview, Sharon Olds mentioned that after hearing a talk about Emily Dickinson, she suddenly flashed upon a vision of Emily Dickinson's naked foot. It occurred to her for the first time that Emily Dickinson actually had soles and toes and ankles. This image helped her feel more connected to Emily Dickinson and her work.

Sylvia Plath had a belly button. Sappho had a pancreas. Jane Austen had knees.

Think about some of your favorite writers. Imagine their toenails, their shoulder blades, their lungs, their thighs. Write about what you see. How does it feel to imagine these beloved writers in such a basic human light?

When you write, don't deny your own body to your readers. Let them under your skin. Show them the heart muscle we all share.

Senses

The FDA tells us to eat five servings of fruits and vegetables a day. As writers, we need to be sure to include all five senses in our daily writing diet. Our most sacred imperative as writers is to keep our senses open. Being present in the world, soaking it all in, will bring vibrancy to both our daily lives and our work.

It is said that God is in the details. Those details can be found only through the body, through the senses. The more vivid and specific we are on the page, the more our writing will have lasting resonance. Sensory writing engages the reader in a way that dry, intellectual writing never can. Let your readers smell what your characters smell. Let your words create a sensory hologram that the reader can step into and look around and feel and taste.

Right now, wherever you are, tune in to your senses. What do you see around you? Look closely. Notice the play of light on the telephone, the furry layer of dust on top of the books, the different degrees of green on the ficus tree. What scent is in the air—wafts of honeysuckle, french fries, armpits? What can you hear—the hum of a fan, the wind rattling the screen, the drip of the leaky faucet in the next room, classical music swelling from the speakers? What textures can you reach out and touch—smooth sheets of paper, sharp pencil tips, nubby chenille pillows? Is there a taste in your mouth—whispers of breakfast, toothpaste, sleep? Write down as many sensory impressions as you can. Choose a few and take them further; see how specific, how expansive you can be with sensory language.

Try to include all five senses on every page you write. This will not always be appropriate or possible, but it is something to keep in mind (and body) as a good way to properly nourish your work.

First Taste, Last Taste

At first all they want is watermelon,
big bites, spitting out the black seeds
while the red pulp melts in their mouths.
They eat it on the ground, their wings
resting moplike behind them . . .
BARBARA RAS, from "Angels on Holiday"

Imagine you are an angel, embodied for the first time. Each sensation is fresh and surprising to you. You have never tasted anything in your celestial life and are eager to test out your new earthly taste buds.

Pick up a piece of fruit. Eat it slowly, carefully (or madly, recklessly, depending on how your angel-self is moved to proceed). How would fruit taste to someone who has never tasted before? Describe the flavors that are unleashed on your newborn tongue.

Now, imagine some time has passed and you know you are about to return to the numinous realm. You are given the chance to have anything you want for your last meal, as lavish as you desire. What would you want your last flavors on earth to be? Write about the meal in detail.

Scent

There are few scents more heavenly than an orange grove in blossom. Or a peach tree in the sun. What are some of your favorite smells? Your least favorite smells?

Diane Ackerman writes, "One of the real tests of writers, especially poets, is how well they write about smells. If they can't describe the scent of sanctity in a church, can you trust them to describe the suburbs of the heart?"

On paper, try to describe the scent of your house. A childhood friend's house. Your closet. Your lover's armpit. Your child's scalp. The garbage can in your kitchen. The rain.

Think of how certain scents can cause memories to come rushing back. Walking through a deli, you catch a whiff of dill pickle brine and are suddenly transported back to your Aunt Frieda's kitchen when you were five years old and helped her put up the cucumbers from her garden. What scents trigger memories for you? How precisely can you capture scent on paper?

Touch

. . . a baby
any baby
your baby is
the
most perfect human thing you can ever touch
translucent
and I want you to think about   touching
and being touched by this most perfect thing
this pear tree blossom
this mouth these leafy hands these genitals
like petals
a warm scalp resting against your cheek
fruit's warmth
beginning—

ALICIA OSTRIKER, from "Propaganda Poem:
Maybe for Some Young Mamas"

What is the most perfect thing, human or not, you've ever touched? Not perfect to the eye. Perfect to the fingers, to the skin. Write about it.

Write about something soft. Something rough. Something wet. Something sticky. Something smooth. Something jagged. Any texture you can think of. Don't just say "soft"—show how soft the thing is. Paint a true tactile picture.

Have someone put a mystery object in a paper bag. Put your hand in without looking and feel the object. Write about it. Not about what you think the object is, even if you are pretty sure you know. Write about the sensation of touching it. Describe on the page how it feels to touch the object. Let the reader feel what you feel.

Eyesight

Who is the apple of your eye? What do you like to feast your eyes upon?

As writers, we need to keep our eyes open, our vision fresh. The whole world is our eye-apple. Everything is a potential vision banquet.

A typical kindergarten homework exercise is a color walk. The child is told to walk around her house and find as many things as she can that are, say, yellow. It is an exercise in seeing, in awareness, in deep attention. We can learn much from exercises for children; seeing through a five-year-old's eyes can help keep our vision fresh, our perspective humble. When we return to our childhood, we can let ourselves—and our vision—blossom all over again.

Choose a color. Walk around your house, or around your neighborhood, and find everything you can in that color. Keep a list. Train your eyes to notice all the subtle differences of shade and tone.

Go for a shadow walk. Write about all the shadows you find.

Go for a shape walk. Look for things that are triangular, square, ovoid.

Think up your own vision walk. What do you want to discover?

Always keep your eyes peeled. When you are a writer, you are in constant dialogue with the world around you. You need to look it straight in the eye.

Listening

No more the shrill voices
that cried Need Need
from the cold pond, bladed
and urgent as new grass

Now it is the crickets
that say Ripe Ripe
slurred in the darkness, while the plums

dripping on the lawn outside
our window, burst
with a sound like thick syrup
muffled and slow
MARGARET ATWOOD, from "Late August"

Writing involves listening. Deep listening. We need to quiet ourselves so we can hear the world around us in a true, clear way.

Close your eyes. Take a few deep breaths, and take a moment to center yourself. Now listen. Try to be aware of all the levels of sound swarming around you—the hum of the computer, the caw of the crows outside, the surprising thump of the water heater, the soft whoosh of cars driving by, your own heartbeat throbbing in your ears. . . .

Susan Griffin writes, *"We take these sounds as testimony: violin, skin, tongue, reed exist. Our bodies know these testimonies as beauty."* Let the audible testimony of the world around you sink into your body. When you are ready, open your eyes and write down what you heard.

When we open our senses, we also can open up our sense of playfulness. Choose a sound, and let yourself come up with wild possibilities for what could be causing it. That lawn mower whirring down the street could be a bunch of giants sewing leather capes, a washing machine full of keys, a gazillion crickets rubbing their legs together. . . .

The Articulate Body

It was seeing the way they waited, with a patient
wistfulness for any attention Celia might chance to offer,
boys who before had not wanted anything from a girl,
that defeated us finally: Celia, in impartial imperious
command, standing among them, her hands fixed like
delicate fan clasps upon her jutting hips, her mouth small
and yet full and piquant, like two sections of an orange.
JOAN CHASE, from *During the Reign of the Queen of Persia*

The body doesn't lie. When we write about a person, real or
fictional, it is important to capture that person's body language—
how she holds her mouth when she's upset, what she does with her
hands when she's bored, whether she slumps in a chair or sits like
she has a steel-bar spine. The language of the body is often more
illuminating than spoken dialogue, which doesn't always express
the character's true feelings.

Choose an emotional state—anger, grief, surprise, joy. Now
write a scene in which a character experiences and communicates
this emotion by using her posture, her gestures, her facial expressions
alone. Don't write any dialogue; don't use the words *angry* or *joyful;*
find a way to let the character's body articulate what she is feeling.

Synesthesia

We bought figs for breakfast, immense thin-skinned
ones. They broke in one's fingers and tasted of wine and
honey. Why is the northern fig such a chaste fair-haired
virgin, such a soprano? The melting contraltos sing
through the ages.

KATHERINE MANSFIELD, from *The Journal of Katharine Mansfield*

When we can hear figs sing in different octaves, we know something wild is going on. Synesthesia, or a blending of the senses, is a wonderful tool that's always at our writerly disposal. The word comes from the Greek *syn*, meaning "together," and *aisthenesthai*, meaning "to perceive." When we see music, for example, or smell the color blue or hear sugar sneeze, we are tapping into our synesthetic capacities, breaking down our own boundaries of perception. Synesthesia is a great way to bring a freshness, a sense of surprise, to our work.

Try your own hand at synesthesia. What sounds can you taste? What scents can you see? What textures can you smell? Be playful. Create all kinds of crazy juxtapositions.

Fruitflesh Meditation: Blackberries

From a distance, a blackberry looks tiny, simple, easy to comprehend. Up close, though, it is much more complex. Its small body is made up of many little sacs of fruit, like a many-nippled breast or a many-breasted goddess. It's amazing how much juice can come out of such a small fruit. Juice that leaves a lasting stain.

Take a while to look at your blackberry. Notice all of its nooks and crannies, its multiply pulped body. Squeeze some of the dark juice out onto your fingers, and lick it off. Pop the berry into your mouth. Don't swallow until the fruit has revealed its many layers of flavor.

When you first start a project, sometimes the subject you're writing about may seem simple, easy to encapsulate. Take a closer look. Let yourself discover all the nuances of the subject, all the little details and wrinkles you may not have noticed right away. Give yourself time to find your story's true contours, its true flavors, the juice that will leave a deep impression.

PART FOUR

Branches

The song the world sings day after day
isn't made of feathers, and the song a bird pours
itself into is tough as a branch
growing with the singer and the singer's delight.

SUSAN MITCHELL,
from "Havana Birth"

Once our words are centered in our fruitflesh, we can begin to branch out into broader, wilder realms of imagination. As the scope of our writing grows, so will our delight.

Fruitflesh Meditation: Pineapple

A pineapple is a trickster. A pineapple doesn't take itself seriously, despite its rough, spiny skin. Just look at its wild green hair! The flesh inside sometimes has a bit of a bite, like the most effective humor.

Cut a pineapple in half, from top to bottom, into two "boats." Score the flesh on both sides so it will come out in easy chunks. Use an outrageously colored paper umbrella to spear each piece into your mouth, or dig your fingers into the fibrous fruit, smoosh your face into the slick curve of it, gnaw at the last sweet shreds. Let the fruit tickle your throat on its way down. Put the empty "boat" on your head, and see how long you can walk around before it tumbles off.

Be playful with your writing. Let yourself be wild! You have permission to be silly, both on and off the page.

A Berry Entire

There are times when I want to be stained,
marked all over by berry wine, baptized,
mouth, fingers, chin and neck, between my toes,
up my legs like the wine-makers of Jerez
who walk round and round in tubs
of berries all day, who return then
to their homes at night wreathed
in berry halos, heady with ripe flower
bouquets dizzy with bees, their bodies
painted, perfumed by purple sun syrup,
their breath elderberry delicious.
. . . .
I want to be so immersed, so earth-wined myself
that I'm mistaken for a berry entire.

PATTIANN ROGERS, from "Berry Renaissance"

What fruit do you want to be mistaken for?

What kind of fruit lives inside you now? If you could peel back your skin like tangerine rind, what would you find underneath? The hard flesh of a coconut? The moist sweetness of a mango? The dark tang of a blackberry?

What kind of fruitflesh do you as a writer want to claim?

Choose a fruit that resonates with you, a fruit that expresses some aspect of who you are or who you want to become. If you can't decide upon a singular fruit, create a hybrid—a lemon-melon, a papaya-pomegranate-plum. Give it a new name.

Write "I am a guava" (or "currant" or "velvet sugar muscle" or whatever fruit calls you). Juice yourself—explore your flavor, your fragrance, your layers of texture and color. Create your own fruitflesh (wo)manifesto. Be juicy and specific.

Fruit Salad Body

There are many tigers in one lemon.

AMANDA BERENGUER, from "el limon," translated by Gayle Brandeis

Sometimes we don't feel as whole as a mango. Just as a dozen tigers can live inside a lemon, sometimes a whole fruit salad can live under our skin. You might feel like you have sour oranges in your knees and grape clusters in your brain and a watermelon stuck in your throat. Maybe your lungs are full of cherries. Write about the different flavors that live in different regions of your body. Again, don't go by how things look (i.e., your breasts are shaped like papayas) but by how they feel from the inside out.

You don't have to limit yourself to fruit. What flora and fauna live inside your body? Do you have monkeys in your stomach and petunias in your heels? Are your breasts the wings of birds, resting? Start with real, felt experience, and name it metaphorically.

For fun, write down a bunch of nouns on separate little slips of paper—lightbulb, parsnip, woolen sock—and put them in a bowl. Then write down a bunch of body parts on other slips of paper—pancreas, elbows, vulva—and put them in another bowl. Pick out a noun and then a body part and put them together. The results will be wild—airplane spleen, coconut spine, zebra tonsil, pillow toe. See what you can do with these pairings. Write a list of them, or choose just one noun and one body part and write a poem, story, or essay with the pairing as the title. Find a way to make somatic sense—or nonsense!—out of the two random words.

Body Maps

Think of those wonderful charts of fruit, cross sections where each bit of skin and seed and stem is labeled. Think of botanical illustrations of flowers—the stamen, the pistil, the petals, each bright and distinct. Maps of gorgeous fruitflesh.

Do the same for your body. Get a big roll of butcher paper. Roll out enough of it to lie down on. Have someone you trust trace around the outline of your body with a pencil or marker. Stand up. How does it feel to see your own outline? This is you, the edge of you. Fill yourself in.

Have fun with this. You could write a list on your arm of all the things your arms do; you could draw lips wherever you like to be kissed; you could put random words all over yourself. You are an orchard, a garden. Are your thighs underground yams, your belly a ripe plum, your breasts birds of paradise?

Name all of your various bodily territories, map out your different regions. Or you could use the butcher paper to unbutcher yourself, to remind yourself that your body is whole and perfect the way it is. You could write one long word that covers the length of your body, a word that expresses how you feel, or want to feel, about yourself. Hang this life-sized self-portrait on your wall when you're done so you can always remember that your body is someplace worth traveling to.

Strange Seizures

People love pretty much the same things best. A writer looking for subjects inquires not after what he loves best, but after what he alone loves at all. Strange seizures beset us. Frank Conroy loves his yo-yo tricks, Emily Dickinson

her slant of light; Richard Seltzer loves the glistening
peritoneum, Faulkner the muddy bottom of a little girl's
drawers visible when she's up a pear tree. "Each student
of ferns," I read, "will have his own list of plants that
for some reason or another stir his emotions."
ANNIE DILLARD, from *The Writing Life*

What "strange seizures" beset you? What do you love that no
one else in the world—as far as you know—even takes a second
look at? A certain kind of stone? Earlobes? Old etiquette books?
The treads of shoes? What peculiar things amaze and amuse you?

Plumb your own quirks. Choose an object or image that inex-
plicably tickles you, a thing that causes you to gape. Capture it on
paper; let your wonder shine through simply in the way you
describe the thing. Annie Dillard goes on to write, "You were made
and set here to give voice to this, your own astonishment." When
you share your astonishment, your readers are almost sure to be
astonished as well.

Morphing

Imagine what it would be like to be a papaya, a cherry, a
bunch of grapes. Try to sense how it feels to be alive inside true
fruitflesh. We can conceive of what it feels like to live in other bod-
ies because we live in our own bodies. Our nerves, our senses, allow
us to empathize in a deep, visceral way.

Write about how it would feel to live inside a body completely
unlike your own. How would it feel to be a large man with a beard? A
conjoined twin? A boy with a hollow chest and a weak chin?

A fun way to try to enter another person's skin is to go to a
thrift shop. Buy an item of clothing and wear it. Imagine who the

clothes used to belong to. Reconstruct the person's body from her dress. What breastbone once filled the cloth? What belly button? Imagine the person's body fully. How did she feel in these clothes? How did she move? How did she feel naked? Spend the day as this other person. Don't be condescending. Do it openly, with compassion. Fully imagine this person's life, her history. Write about your experience.

Our physical imagination allows us to morph into all kinds of incredible life forms on the page, not just other people. How would it feel to live inside a fish? A cat? A cactus? A creature that doesn't even exist in the real world? Let your body's imagination run wild, but try to keep your writing grounded in actual sensation so the reader has a touchstone. Let yourself branch out inside someone else's skin.

Mystery Fruits

We are surrounded by mystery. It is fun and often profound to create ritual that acknowledges and celebrates how much we do not know.

When my husband goes grocery shopping, sometimes he brings home a mystery fruit. He picks a fruit he doesn't recognize, a single fruit, and surprises me with it. The kids and I always devour the mysterious treat with great anticipation and ceremony.

This ritual started a few years ago. We were very poor at the time, so exotic fruit was a huge splurge. It was well worth it, though. We savored each bite of pepino or sapote or pineapple quince or whatever mystery fruit my husband happened to snare.

I buy mystery fruit now when I see something particularly intriguing. The kids like to join in as well. Yesterday my daughter chose a horned melon, or kiwiano, at the store. It was bright orange, the size of a potato, with spikes all over it. We had no idea what it would look like inside. Since it was called a melon, we figured its flesh would be like cantaloupe or maybe canary melon (a mystery fruit from the week before). We were startled when I cut the melon in half. It looked like it was filled with frog spawn or alien goo. The hollow melon was swimming with seeds encased in a pale green slime. They tasted vaguely like cucumber and left an oily coat on our tongues. Definitely mysterious.

It's energizing for us as writers to keep expanding our horizons, to keep trying new things, new tastes. It's important for us to keep surprising ourselves. We allow the scope of our writing to flower when we open the scope of our experience. Try a fruit you've never tasted before. See what it unleashes on your tongue and on the page.

Milk Tongue

THE WORD *PLUM*
The word plum *is delicious*

pout and push, luxury of
self-love, and savoring murmur

full in the mouth and falling
like fruit

taut skin
pierced, bitten, provoked into
juice, and tart flesh

question
and reply, lip and tongue
of pleasure.
HELEN CHASIN

What words are delicious to you? What words do you love for the sound of them alone, for how they feel when you speak them out loud? The poet Donald Hall calls the feel of words in the mouth "milk tongue."

When we first learned to speak, all words were delicious. Our milky baby tongues wrapped themselves around vowels and consonants with visceral exuberance. We can recapture that same joyful, playful experimentation with language and sound, both on the page and in our mouths.

Write down a list of words you love to say, or even made-up words you love the sound of. Speak them, sing them out loud. Let them bloom slowly on your tongue. Let your whole body reverberate with your own private pleasure language.

Naming

Adam naming the fruit
after the creation of fruit,
his tongue tickling
the crimson lips of the pomegranate,
the tip of his penis licking
the cheeks of the peach,
quince petals in his hair,
his blue arms full of plums,
his legs wrapped around watermelons,
dandling pumpkins on his fatherly knees,
tomatoes heaped around him in red pyramids . . .

peach
peach
peach
peach
peach

he sighs

to kingdom come.
ERICA JONG, from "Fruits and Vegetables"

If you had to rename everything in the world, how would you do it?

In most indigenous tongues, there is a deep connection between landscape and language, between word and body, word and movement. In her essay "Land Speaking," in the book *Speaking for the Generations: Native Writers on Writing*, Jeannette C. Armstrong talks about the Okanagan word for dog. The word, *kekwep*, itself is an experience. The first syllable, *kek*, means "happening upon a small (thing)." The second syllable, *wep*, means something akin to "sprouting profusely (as in fur)."

Armstrong writes, "When you say the Okanagan word for dog, you don't 'see' a dog image, you summon an experience of a little furred life, the exactness of which is known only by its interaction with you or something. Each such little furred life is then significant in its own unique way."

Try renaming a couple of things with these ideas in mind. How would you rename apple or pencil or belly based upon your own experience of it? How would you rename yourself?

Looking at the names of fruit cultivars is another way to find language made more precise. There are dozens of varieties of gooseberries—Abundance, Careless, Invicta, Remarka, Spinefree, Yellow Rough, just to name a few of them. Don't these names make each type of berry seem more specific? Can't you taste them each distinctly?

Flowers have cultivars, too. Varieties of hybrid tea roses include Big Apple, Chrysler Imperial, Dolly Parton, Fragrant Cloud. Can you imagine how each one looks? How do you think each one wears its name?

Name your own cultivars. Try naming different varieties of bread—not rye or whole wheat, but *seed sponge, pillow bite*. Name different types of kisses. Different ways of walking. Different aspects of yourself. How can you name the subtle differences you find in the world in a precise, specific way, a way that has true resonance in the body?

Dictionary Poems

COMFIT
(13c): a candy consisting of a piece
of fruit, a root (as licorice), a nut, or
a seed coated and preserved with sugar

I want to roll you
in sugar. I want
you crusted sweet.
I want the grains
to pack into the curl
of your ear, glitter
from your eyelashes,
fill your belly button
like lint. I want to coat
each of your limbs
with a second sucrose skin.
I want to preserve each
honeyed inch of you.
I want to love you
until my teeth ache.

Every day for almost two months, just for fun, I looked through the dictionary, found a word I had never heard of before, and wrote a poem about it. I chose words with sounds or meanings I found particularly evocative, particularly ripe for exploration. I was amazed by what these words unlocked in me. Some of the poems that resulted were intensely personal; others had nothing to do with me at all. *Comfit* was one of my favorites.

Give this a try. Crack open the dictionary, and find a new word. See what branches out from it.

Spells

Let the sun flash through maple flowers tasseled
like earrings   through small paned windows
touch their peach duvet   peach flannel sheets
Let karmas of cramped children   stunting parents
give room
Shut the sad brain   let it be skin only
Draw a circle around their cherrywood bed for this hour

Let the peach cave in a cave burnish away their imperfections
Let their eyes be slits   discriminating
Let hands soften   hips unknot   backs let go
old compressions
Let failures spice their soft bellies   their tinder
take fire
SONDRA ZEIDENSTEIN, from "The One Dream (A Spell)"

Science is beginning to acknowledge the physical effects of prayer, the reverberations of the words we send out into the world. We invoke a lot of magic when we call words onto the page.

One way for us to consciously tap into this magic is to write little spells and blessings. When we broadcast our own wishes for peace or healing—for ourselves, for the people we love, for the world at large—we create space for those things to happen. Use Sondra Zeidenstein's poem as a model, and begin each sentence with *Let*. What prayers do you want to send through the responsive air? What blessings do you want to unleash? You can wish big, of course, but keep the language grounded in reality: the soft bellies, the peach duvet, the cherrywood bed.

Muse

> *I follow the scent of a woman*
> *Melon heavy*
> *Ripe with joy*
> *Inspiring me*
> *To rip great holes in the night*
> *So the sun blasts through*
> RITA MAE BROWN, from "Dancing the Shout to the True Gospel
> or The Song Movement Sisters Don't Want Me to Sing"

Do you have a muse? Is there a person in your life, real or imagined, who inspires you in your creative work? If not, you can always create one to help guide you through your darker times.

What would your muse look like? Would she be a fairy that flits around your head as you write, or would she be a large, plush woman who cheers you on from the sidelines? Close your eyes, and invite her to introduce herself. What does her voice sound like? What does she have to tell you? When you are ready, bring her to the page. You may want to draw or paint her as well as describe her with words so you can keep her image nearby while you write. You may also want to write an invocation, a small phrase or sentence (even something as simple as "O Muse, enter me!") that will conjure her up when you need her.

Masks

Sitting on the stool at the mirror,
she applied a peachy foundation that seemed to hold her down,
to trap her,
as if we never would have noticed what flew among us unless
  it was
weighted and bound in its mask.

Toi Derricotte, from "Christmas Eve: My Mother Dressing"

We all wear masks. Whether we slather our faces with shades of plum and cherry or force ourselves to smile when we are anything but happy, there are times when each of us masks our true skin, our true self. Sometimes a mask can be freeing. At a costume party, when our real face is covered, we can show parts of ourselves that are normally hidden. In our real lives, though, the masks we construct to protect ourselves can easily trap us, hold us down.

We can wear masks as writers, also. These masks can be fun; we can clothe ourselves in the faces of our characters, take on personas wildly different from our own, disappear into new identities, new skins. Sometimes, however, our writing masks can cover our own voices, amplifying them beyond recognition with bravado, muffling them under layers of fear. The page is a safe place to take off these masks, to be naked, bare faced, bare voiced, real. When we write, we can relax our facial muscles, let them soften into their natural state as the words flow through us.

What masks do you wear, in your life and in your work? Imagine them hanging from a wall, like those at a costume shop. Describe each one in detail. Are there any you particularly love? Any you want to get rid of?

Now write about your true face. Don't use any value judgments. Describe yourself with clear, compassionate eyes. How can you let your real face, your real voice, shine through your words?

Inverting the World

TASTELESS MELONS (MELONES INSPIDI)

But you can see, can't you, how I've
inverted the world, turning it in
to myself? First the green rim,
then flesh, and then a network of glistening
seeds, each one a nascent universe.
My nature? Cold and humid, but contained
by rind as dry as cantaloupe's.
Some days, so many strands draw in
on my attention, I forget to say,
it's nice, the way you touch my shoulder.
Tasteless melons have their danger: If I
cause you pain, it's because I forget
my surface. How pale and rough I must
seem to you, all ribs, a lifeless star.

JODY GLADDING

Sometimes, even when all our masks are stripped away, our inner selves still feel out of step with our external selves. We can be naturally quiet in the world, for instance, and comfortable in that quietness, while inside we can be filled with music, glimmering and multifaceted as a kaleidoscope. One of the reasons we write is to let that music out, to spill those colors onto the page, give them voice.

What would you look like if your inner self seeped out onto your face and body? Would you sprout wings? Fangs? Would you have one purple hand, one plaid? Would your hair become sugar floss, moss, copper wire? Your breasts fountains or turtle shells? Would you be afraid of how you looked, or would you be happy, like you were seeing the real you for the first time? Write your inner self out on the page; coax your imagination onto your skin.

Meaning

A poem should be palpable and mute
As a globed fruit.
ARCHIBALD MACLEISH, from "Ars Poetica"

It is easy to get bogged down in meaning when we write. We want our words to have lasting resonance, after all. We want them to touch upon important things—Truth, Beauty, what it means to be human. The best way we can express these things, though, is by offering specific, tangible, palpable examples. We can say what we want to say in our work without spelling it out in capital letters. As Archibald Macleish later writes, "A poem should not mean / but be." Let your story or poem "be," and the meaning will unfold from that be-ing.

Choose a big issue—Liberty, Justice, the Meaning of Life. Now pick something concrete—apple, beach ball, xylophone. Put these two things together as a title—Liberty Apple; Beach Ball of Justice; Xylophonia: The Meaning of Life—and find a way to express the big idea by using the tangible object as a metaphor, an illustration. Be sure to include your senses, not just your thoughts, as you write: "The bars of the xylophone are each a different color—lemon yellow, pea green, pink like a tongue. If you rub your hand along the edge of the instrument, the graded lengths feel choppy, discordant, against your palm, but as soon as you trip the rubber mallet across the metal, the notes rise up in harmony. . . ."

A Slip of the Pen

*Meaning, if it existed at all, was unstable and could not
survive the slightest reshuffling of letters. One gust of
wind and Santa became Satan. A slip of the pen and
pears turned into pearls.*

LORRIE MOORE, from "The Nun of That"

The English language can be so funny. *Waffle* looks like *raffle*
but sounds like *awful*. *Plough* sounds like *plow*, while *slough* can
sound like *sluff*. *Stressed* spelled backward is *desserts; evil* spelled
backward is *live.*

Play around with some of the oddities of language. Write a
sentence backward and see how it looks. *Skool ti woh ees dna drawkcab
ecnetnes a etirw.* Change each word in a sentence—*Charge peach worm
inn egg semblance*—to a word that is implied in the original one, either
by spelling or by sound. Break words down into new phonemes—
phone could be "p-hone," *Bakelite* could be "Bah-kee-lit-ay." Create
your own nonsense language à la "Jabberwocky." Seek out fun typos
(like "Spicy Human Beans" on the menu at the Hunan restaurant),
and write a poem or story about them. Don't worry about making
sense; it's nearly impossible to when doing these exercises! Just have
fun messing around with all the bizarre and wondrous possibilities
our alphabet has to offer. Words are what fill our writerly toy box. We
should play with them as much as possible! Goofing around with
sound and syntax and spelling is a great way to limber up our writing
muscles, to get more supple in the ways we string together words.

Sensory Confusion

*It was as if he were trying to swallow a cherry but found
he was only the size of the stem of the cherry. His mouth
received and was explored by some immensity. It became
more and more immense while he waited. All knowledge
of the rest of his body and the feeling in it would leave
him; he would not find it possible to describe his position
in the bed, where his legs were or his hands; his mouth
alone felt and it felt enormity. Only the finest, frailest
thread of his own body seemed to exist, in order to
provide the mouth. He seemed to have the world on his
tongue. And it had no taste—only size.*

EUDORA WELTY, from "Music from Spain"

Sometimes our fruitflesh plays funny tricks on us. This often
happens when our minds get out of sync with our bodies, be it
through fever, illness, fatigue, or certain substances. Sometimes we
hallucinate—seeing, hearing, feeling things that aren't really there.
Sometimes one part of our body engulfs our perception; our tongue
feels huge in our mouth, our body becomes all lung. Other times
our senses just get confused. Once I almost got into a car crash
because I saw a bald head split neatly in half in the car next to
mine. It took me a moment to realize it was really two bare feet
pressed against the passenger window, parting.

Think of a time your senses played a trick on you—the time
you saw water vapor rippling in the desert during a hiking trip or
felt a new set of lips growing on the palm of your hand at a Grateful
Dead concert or imagined each strand of your hair could sing during
a fever. Did you find this sensory confusion scary or liberating?
How can you capture the strangeness of the experience?

Whirling

Some trees, like the maple, have small winged fruits that whirl like helicopters as they fall from the branch, drilling their seed down into the ground. Whirling can be a fruitful act for writers as well.

Rumi, the thirteenth-century mystic poet, composed thousands of poems while he whirled, one palm turned up to face the heavens, one turned down to face the earth. "Turn as the earth and moon turn," he tells us, "circling what they love. / Whatever circles comes from the center."

The experience of writing can be just as dizzying, just as centering, as the whirl itself. Annie Dillard writes, "The sensation of writing a book is the sensation of spinning, blinded by love and daring."

See if you can consciously write in a way that captures revolution, circularity, the whirl. Perhaps your words can literally circle the page. Or you can begin and end each sentence or each paragraph with the same word. You could also get up and whirl around until the world blurs, then sit back down to write while the room is still spinning. Find a way to let your writing tap into the revolution that is happening right now in the atoms that make up your body, the steady revolution of our planet around the sun. Our basic state of being is the whirl. Just as the maple fruit dances its seed down into the earth, so can this circular movement plant many seeds in your own work.

Fruitflesh Meditation: Pear

The pear is a sensitive fruit. Its peel is easily bruised, easily broken through. Its core is a delicate spine of filaments. The pear is no weakling, though. Its strength lies in its vulnerability. It knows who it is and isn't afraid to acknowledge its own frailties or its own sweet power.

Hold a ripe pear. Feel how present it is in its voluptuous form. Smell its musky perfume. Run your tongue along the skin. Take a bite. See how easily the skin curls and opens beneath your teeth. Notice the texture of the flesh in your mouth. It is smooth but grainy—flesh that doesn't deny the rougher textures of life. Swallow the slender core. Let its spider web threads hold your own sweet, fragile dreams together.

When you write, let yourself be vulnerable. Don't deny the coarse grains of your experience. Your open self-awareness can give you true and lasting strength.

PART FIVE

Leaves

Leaves are verbs that conjugate the seasons.
GRETEL ERLICH,
from *The Solace of Open Spaces*

We cycle through many seasons in our lives. We may favor the leafy green seasons, the lush fragrant seasons, but we also need to honor those seasons of change, of dryness, those seasons where we feel stripped bare. If we want to bring our whole self to the page, we need to explore our darkness, our shadow, as well as our light.

Fruitflesh Meditation: Papaya

Papayas can be pear shaped or round like avocados, their skins green, yellow, orange, or rose. Their flesh is slick and smooth and generous, with a shade that ranges from a rich yellow to a dusky orange-pink. Papayas are sometimes delicate and flowery in flavor, sometimes sour with musk. The core of the fruit is filled with black, glistening seeds.

Slice a papaya in half. Note the seeds gleaming dark in the central cavity. They may not look edible, but they are. Pick one up, slide it between your fingers. It is softer than you imagined, isn't it?

We all carry darkness inside our bodies. We all have secrets, fears, anger, and pain hiding somewhere inside our cells. Writing is a safe place to acknowledge our own darkness, to come to terms with it and let it go.

Put the dark seed in your mouth. Feel its gelatinous coating. Darkness is shrouded sometimes, slippery, not easy to enter. Bite through the coating into the seed itself. Let its peppery flavor spill over your tongue.

You are free to write about your darkness. You are free to taste and release the things that scare you most.

Slice a bit of the papaya flesh, and eat that, too. Feel its integrity, its solid softness. Your body has just as much integrity, just as much soft strength. Your body will support you as you venture into your own darkness on the page.

Miraculous Fruit

When Africans chew a berry they call "miraculous fruit,"
it becomes impossible to taste anything sour: lemons taste
sweet, sour wine tastes sweet, rhubarbs taste sweet.
Anything off-puttingly sour suddenly becomes delicious.

Diane Ackerman, from *A Natural History of the Senses*

Writing is a miraculous fruit. It doesn't necessarily make sour things sweet, but it can make them easier to swallow, to bear. We can tap into the most painful experiences in our lives—our most embarrassing moments, our deepest encounters with fear and grief—and face them, transform them, release them on the page.

Think of a sour moment in your life that you've been afraid to confront, afraid to write about. If the experience is still too raw, you can always enter it sideways. Write about the experience from the third person—use *she* instead of *I* ("she began to have night sweats," "she picked up the phone in the middle of the night"). Taking the *I* away often frees us to see the situation more clearly, to observe nuances we might otherwise overlook. Sometimes when we fictionalize events, we can come to a deeper place of truth.

Even if you do remove the *I* from your telling, don't remove your body. Through "her" body, let your body tell its tale. How did your body respond to fear, to pain? Take the reader fully inside the skin of the experience.

Writing is a courageous act; we can write ourselves into wholeness by facing our darkness on the page. The sour may remain sour even after the writing of it, but it probably won't continue to hold the same power. Have you ever tried a sour apple Warhead candy or an especially pucker-inducing lemon drop? When you first put one in your mouth, it's almost unbearably sour, but after you get over the initial shock and cringe, it begins to turn sweet on your tongue. When we see that we have power over difficult subject matter, it loses its bitter edge, becomes all the more palatable.

Eating Fear

Why won't Eve eat of the fruit?
Didn't Eve have a hand to reach out with,
fingers with which to make a fist;
didn't Eve have a stomach to feel hunger with,
a tongue to feel thirst,
a heart with which to love?

But then why won't Eve eat of the fruit?

Why would Eve merely suppress her wishes,
regulate her steps?
Subdue her thirst?
. . . .
because Eve has eaten of the fruit
there is joy, because she has eaten there is joy,
joy, joy—
Eating of the fruit, Eve made a heaven of the earth.
Eve, if you get hold of the fruit
don't ever refrain from eating.
TASLIMA NASRIN, from "Eve Oh Eve," translated from the Bengali
by Carolyne Wright and Mohammad Nurul Huda

What holds you back from your own creative fruition? Memories of being told you aren't "good enough"? Your own fear of failure or success? Fear of being swept away by the creative process? What makes the leaves of your writing sometimes begin to dry up just as soon as they start to unfurl?

Life is too short for us to deny our own dreams, to sidestep our passions. Inventory your fears, your deep blocks, the things that keep you from following your own bliss as a woman and a writer. Can you give these things flesh? Write about what your blocks look like, feel like. Are they actual blocks—dark slabs of wood, full of knots and whorls? Maybe one is a chunk of food that gets stuck in your throat and makes it difficult for you to breathe freely. If so, what food would this block, this fear, be? A prickly pear, maybe, full of forbidding spikes? A coconut with a seemingly impenetrable shell? Get the actual food item that represents your fear, and tear into it with your teeth, devour it with all your heart. Show yourself that you can digest this fear, that you can let it pass through you, that it can nourish you with its intense flavor. You may be surprised to find that what lies under the hard rind of fear can sometimes be moist and delicious.

Whenever you feel the call of creation, whenever you catch a glimpse of the fruit of your potential, don't ever, ever refrain from eating. Dive right in. Let yourself get sweet and sticky with it.

A Bit Dodgy

"You're not a poetess, I hope," said the English geologist next to her. "We had a poetess here last month, and things got a bit dodgy here for the rest of us."

"Really." After the soup, there was risotto with squid ink.

"Yes. She kept referring to insects as 'God's typos' and then she kept us all after dinner one evening so she could read from her poems, which seemed to consist primarily of the repeating line 'the hairy kiwi of his balls.'"
LORRIE MOORE, from "Terrific Mother"

Sometimes we avoid writing something so we won't offend certain people. Heaven forbid your aunt Gladys finds out that you masturbate or your mom discovers you once tried LSD in college or the head of your department sees you have desires that extend beyond the syllabus you submit at the beginning of each semester!

Don't let worries like this censor your creativity. When we leave aspects of ourselves out of our work, the work is not as robust as it will be if we let our full selves appear on the page.

If people get a little dodgy when you read, well, that just means you're touching a nerve. Your work is powerful enough to make someone squirm. This is a good thing. If you make *yourself* uncomfortable with your work, you know you're really onto something—crossing your own boundaries, sailing into previously uncharted (or previously avoided) territory. Don't worry about embarrassing yourself or offending others. Let the words that want to come, come.

To discover what makes you dodgy, write "I am most afraid to write about . . ." and then write why. You may trick yourself into going straight into the very woods you've been trying to avoid. Remember, you don't need to show this writing to anyone. This is for your own personal exploration and growth. How does it feel to break down your self-imposed barriers?

Embarrassment

We were made fools of.
And the scent of mock orange
drifts through the window.

How can I rest?
How can I be content
when there is still
that odor in the world?
Louise Glück, from "Mock Orange"

Being a person can be embarrassing. We say the "wrong" thing, we open our hearts to people who toss us aside, we get ourselves into all sorts of awkward and humiliating situations. Sometimes a simple scent, a single image, can trigger a memory that causes shame to come flooding back. Writing about the situation can help us rest, can help us be content even in the face of our own tender foolishness.

Think about a time when you were most embarrassed. How did your body respond to the situation? Maybe the tips of your shoulder blades went cold, maybe sweat pooled behind your knees; perhaps your stomach plummeted to your ankles or your heart seemed to freeze midbeat in your chest. Write about the moment with as much clarity as possible, but try to be gentle with yourself; don't beat yourself up all over again. You can even rewrite the scene to exonerate yourself, if you want to. Say that witty retort you thought of three hours after the fact, throw that glass of water in someone's face, walk out of the room with your head held high. When we are able to keep a sense of humor about, and compassion for, our biggest human foibles, it is that much easier to get beyond them and find our own peace.

Pain

Your pain is the breaking of the shell that encloses your understanding. Even as the stone of the fruit must break, that its heart may stand in the sun, so must you know pain.
KAHLIL GIBRAN

In childbirth classes, pregnant women are sometimes instructed to think of each contraction during labor as an "interesting sensation" rather than pain. While this is easier said than done, such advice helps shift our perception so we can open ourselves to the feeling instead of tensing our muscles against it in fear. There does come a point, however, when the sensation can no longer qualify as *interesting*, a point when we can only recognize pain by its true name.

Pain has much to teach us. It has its own vocabulary, its own logic—or lack thereof. Suffering can break us down, but it can also break us open. As in labor, it can cause parts of us to dilate inside, to become more receptive to whatever wants to rush through us. If we don't harden ourselves against it, the ache will help our hearts expand.

In many ways, pain is beyond language, but we can try to penetrate the white-hot center of it with our words. Think of questions your doctor asks—is the sensation dull, throbbing, burning, stabbing? You can use similar terminology, but try not to get too clinical in your language. Write from deep inside the experience; let it sear its way onto the page.

Embracing the Prune

> *And if anyone complains that prunes, even when*
> *mitigated by custard, are an uncharitable vegetable (fruit*
> *they are not), stringy as a miser's heart and exuding a*
> *fluid such as might run in misers' veins who have denied*
> *themselves wine and warmth for eighty years and yet not*
> *given to the poor, he should reflect that there are people*
> *whose charity embraces even the prune.*
> VIRGINIA WOOLF, from *A Room of One's Own*

When we write, our charity needs to embrace even the prune. We need to become pure open channels for every wrinkle, every flavor of life to move through us. It is important to place our prejudices aside and let each character, each idea breathe fully on the page. If we approach our writing subjects—even the "bad guys"—with clarity and compassion, they will be that much more alive, that much more human. No one is a cardboard cutout; no real person is two dimensional. All people have their own fears and hopes, favorite colors, favorite foods, and when we can find these very human traits in others, it makes it that much easier for us to connect on a basic level, even with people and characters we can't stand.

Think of a person you know who rubs you the wrong way or a villainous character from one of your stories. Write a scene from his or her perspective. Try not to color your portrait with your own negative feelings about this person. Your character may remain an evil terror, and you may continue to bristle when the person you know walks by, but your heart (and your creative scope) will probably open as a result of writing from his or her perspective.

Falling

When an apple fell on Sir Isaac Newton's head, he discovered gravity. When I see something fall, I rediscover lightness.

Falling is a moment of loss of control, a moment that breaks through all the constructs of how a person is supposed to behave. It flies in the face of upright society. It reminds me that the body has its own agenda, its own humor and vulnerabilities that the mind has no power over. Think of how the word *fall* is used. We *fall* in love, we *fall* to sleep, we *fall* to pieces, we *fall* into every dark region of the human heart, every place that operates in a subconscious, uncontrolled way. Falling is a subversive, and often hysterical, act. At the same time, it is part of the natural cycle; think about how leaves fall, how they give the tree space for new growth.

When I first learned to ice-skate, the first thing I was taught was how to fall down. It taught me to be less afraid of really falling because I also learned how to get back up. I came to enjoy the thrill of falling, the glittery rush before I hit the hard ice.

As writers, maybe we, too, need to learn how to fall or at least not be so afraid of falling. We don't need to always be upright, in control of what we are writing. We need to let ourselves slip around on language a bit, fall into the well of dreams and sensation that courses underneath.

Try writing with your eyes closed. Let your words slide around the page, wherever they end up. Write with the hand you don't normally write with. How does this affect the content of your work? Try writing on a new surface; use a fat marker on a huge sheet of newsprint. Let yourself be sloppy, careless. Like ice, this new surface can help you slip around, fall into new ways of using language.

Other times, when your work seems to take on its own life, taking you into dark territory you had not planned to explore, let yourself fall into it. It may feel scary, it may feel exhilarating. Just let the tumbling words take you where they need to go. Your fruit-flesh is resilient. You'll be able to get back up.

Blood and Guts

The melon-burst, the tomato-colored splatter—now that's a story. . . .
MARGARET ATWOOD, from "Bad News"

Bodies are fragile. We can be split open, bruised, contused, scraped, gouged, crunched. Many things can happen to us. It is good to recognize this—not so we live in constant fear of the dangers that we face, but so we can connect with our own tenderness, our own vulnerability.

Movies are so filled with images of violence, of gore, of blood and guts, that we become numb to the true consequences of injury. With our words, we can shake ourselves out of numbness; we can help others remember to feel. Unlike in the movies, in writing we are not aiming for sensationalism; we are aiming for true, deep, sensation.

Think of a moment when you experienced or witnessed an injured body—the dead possum that oozed against the road, maybe, or the time you were cutting a bagel and ended up getting a rare glimpse of your own finger bone. Record the moment with as much clarity and detail as possible. It is important for us as writers to be able to look at all aspects of our existence, especially the ones we consider grotesque.

Turning to Pie

*Edgar put his head in his hands. He was suffering from
    nothingness, he explained.
My mother went to the refrigerator and took out a box. She
    poured Edgar a glass of milk and tucked a napkin under
    his chin.
"Are you aware," she said, "that at the end of his life, Jean-
    Paul Sartre renounced existentialism and turned to pie?"
Edgar looked at my mother through his half-empty glass. "What
    do you mean?" he asked.
"Just what I said, of course." She smiled at him and served us
    pie. It was cherry-rhubarb with crumbs on top. My mother
    held a forkful to her mouth. "Heaven," she said.*
JENNY OFFILL, from *Last Things*

My first semester of college, I took a freshman seminar entitled "Construction and Deconstruction of the Self." We seemed to do a lot more deconstructing than constructing that term, stripping ourselves of one belief after another. It was an incredible, life-changing seminar, one that brought into question everything I thought I knew, everything I thought I was. While I was thrilled by this self-dissection, I also found myself suffering from nothingness fairly often, teetering on the verge of existential angst. Nothing seemed solid anymore; nothing seemed to make much sense.

Once again, I was saved by a strawberry. Eventually, whenever I felt myself confronting the Void, I remembered Ms. Sweers's class. I remembered that if I took the time to open my senses, to be fully present in the moment, to focus on the sensation of a berry on my lips, its flavors on my tongue, I could pull myself back from the brink. Whenever I felt ready to drift into nothingness, I'd remember to drench myself in color or see how many sounds I could identify swirling through the dorm, letting my senses give me new, fierce focus. My body became my anchor. It grounded me as I puzzled over who I was. It centered me as I began to reconstruct my Self once again.

When we write, we can sometimes slip into an existential black hole, either inside ourselves or on the page itself. This can make for interesting literature, certainly, but it can also be incredibly disorienting and disconcerting when you're in the middle of it. If you find yourself facing a great maw of emptiness as you write, your senses can provide the perfect escape hatch. Bracing water on the wrists, a strong whiff of peppermint, the heaven of cherry-rhubarb pie can help bring you back to yourself, back to the vivid aliveness of the moment, both on the page and off.

Anger

But I have peeled away your anger
down to its core of love
and look mother
I am
a dark temple where your true spirit rises
beautiful and tough as a chestnut
AUDRE LORDE, from "Black Mother Woman"

Anger often has a fruitful core. Legend tells that the hala tree, native to the Hawaiian Islands, is so abundant as the result of the goddess Pele's rage. Pele, so the story goes, once rowed her canoe ashore, and the boat became entangled in some hala roots. In her anger, she ripped the tree to shreds and tossed the pieces across the island. Everywhere they landed, they sprouted and grew into strong, vibrant trees. Her anger was indeed a fruitful one: the Hawaiian people have used every part of the tree ever since. The pollen is considered an aphrodisiac, the blossoms are used to make leis, the fruit is a great delicacy, the leaves are woven into purses and baskets, the bark and wood and roots are shaped into boats and carvings—all born of a goddess's rage.

Women's anger has traditionally been suppressed. In the past few decades, women writers have thankfully been able to explore and release their rage, but it is still difficult for some of us to acknowledge or express our anger today. Anger is not always a "nice" feeling; it can be an excruciating feeling, but it is often a purifying, cathartic one, an important one for us to own.

How does anger manifest itself in your body—a slow boil in the belly? A fierce burning in the chest? How does anger transform your face, your heart? It is no coincidence that Pele is associated with volcanoes, with the transformative power of fire. If your anger were a goddess, what would she look like? Write about her—describe her hair, her voice, her eyes, her hands. What does she want to say? What gifts can she offer you?

Protest

CROSSING
During the 1933 Nazi
boycott of Jewish businesses,
the grandmother of
theologian Dietrich
Bonhoeffer crossed the line
to buy strawberries from a
Jewish grocer.

Strawberries
after supper tonight
with cream.
Like the first mother
I picked
forbidden fruit,
risking fist and boot.

No paradise, here.
The white father
in a fury lit
the pilot, split
sheep from goat,
soon ashen thunderheads
will float
over Germany.

But tonight,
strawberries.
DEMETRIA MARTINEZ

Sometimes our bodies register protest before our minds can begin to grasp the situation. The simple hunger for strawberries—the desire for sweetness in the face of fury—can lead to acts of dissent we may not otherwise be capable of.

How does protest register in your body? As cry? An ache? A sense of burning in your gut?

Maya Angelou has said, "Protest is an inherent part of my work. You can't just not write about protest themes or not sing about them. It's a part of life. If I don't agree with a part of life, then my work has to address it."

Think about a part of life you don't agree with. It can be small—the way a teacher singles out a certain child for ridicule, for example—or large, such as the imprisonment of dissident poets in China, the destruction of the environment, the increase of hate crimes. Write about this issue; be sure to address the physicality of the situation as well as your intellectual and emotional response to it.

Words have the power to change the world—globally as well as within us. The page can be our utopia, where we create the world we want to live in. It can also be a mirror that reflects the world as it is, shedding light upon the problems we feel need attention. Our writing can incite anger and inspire peace. Writing can be a powerful act of protest in itself.

Bruised Fruit

"Summer Ends Too Soon"

Was the last she said. Beautiful
Maria, Ave Maria. Maria dodging
father's fists—and his. Maria praying
under the table. Maria crooning pain
songs in the bathroom. Maria combing
his sludge out of her hair. Maria
serving masters. Seventeen year

old Maria. Maria, your Lady
of the Kept Secret. Maria dancing
to his temper. Maria washing
her panties in the toilet. Two
days after graduation, Maria
swaying from the limb. Maria,
sweet purple fruit of his sin.
Ave Maria.

LORNA DEE CERVANTES

Women's bodies get hurt. Way too often, women and girls are the subject of abuse and violence. The statistics are staggering: one in three women will be sexually assaulted in her lifetime. We all have friends and sisters who have experienced some sort of abuse if we ourselves have not.

Often when a woman has been abused, it is hard for her to see her body as anything other than a source of pain, fear, and deep shame. The best revenge we can take against this violence is to love and respect our bodies even more. We can't let anyone take away our pleasures, our sensual enjoyment. If we go numb, we give away too much of ourselves. By cutting ourselves off from our bodies, we cut ourselves off from our own real power.

Writing about the body, through the body, can help women who have been abused and attacked begin to reclaim their own bodies as sources of pleasure and joy, can help heal the unthinkable damage that has been done.

Try to write about the ways in which your body, or the body of someone you love, has been hurt. How has this pain affected your relationship with your body? Your creativity? The world at large? Write about the ways in which you can begin to reclaim your body, and all of its sensation and expression, as your own.

Illness

An apple a day keeps the doctor away.
Therefore, I have hung it on strong thread
In the empty space of air
That waits behind the door
Like a square mouth full of trees.

All day now, I rock my chair
And watch the doctor,
A great black crow,
Circling that red globe.

SUSAN FROMBERG SCHAEFFER, from "Proverbs"

Sometimes all the apples in the world can't keep the doctor away. We get sick, sometimes very sick. Writing from the body, from the core of our fruitflesh, can help us explore our relationship with pain, with fear, with vulnerability, with all the physical darkness that illness can unleash.

In her book *Women's Bodies, Women's Wisdom*, Dr. Christiane Northrup suggests that people write dialogues with the part of the body that is causing them problems. She instructs her patients to ask their bodies what they are trying to tell them and write about it in their journals. One woman asked her pelvis what wisdom it was trying to express through her fibroid and heavy menstrual bleeding. She waited for several days until her body responded, "Your periods are symbolic of the way you give yourself away too freely. The heavy bleeding represents your own life's blood draining away."

The messages our bodies send us are often equally symbolic. We sometimes have digestive problems when we can't stomach something in our lives, throat problems when we are having trouble expressing ourselves, eye problems when we are denying our true vision. . . .

What parts of your body are most vulnerable to stress, to illness? What messages is your body trying to send you? Write from the perspective of your migraine, your sore knee, your menstrual cramps. Let your body tell you what it needs. Listen to its requests with love and attention.

Healing

Writing from our fruitflesh not only can help us cope with illness; evidence shows that writing may help heal the body as well. A study published in the *Journal of the American Medical Association* (April 14, 1999) showed that asthma and arthritis patients often improved after writing about stressful events in their lives. Patients who were instructed to write lists of their plans for the day showed only about half as much improvement as those patients who wrote about real, significant events in their lives. Some asthma patients showed increased lung capacity within only two weeks of beginning to write. Writing can open the body, just as the body can open the scope of our writing.

Even when an illness or disability is untreatable, writing can help us heal our problematic relationship with our bodies, and we can come to appreciate our bodies' inherent wisdom in the process.

Cheryl Marie Wade, director of Wry Crips Disabled Women's Theater Group and solo pieces like *A Woman with Juice*, found that through her writing and performance she was able to discover the unique power of her body, which had been severely disfigured by rheumatoid arthritis. In an interview she relates, "By writing about my body and about what I call the 'ugly beauty' of disability, I began to like my body. I do mind the pain and the limitations, but I don't hate the actual physical differences anymore."

Nancy Mairs often writes about how MS has affected her body and her writing. "Forced by the exigencies of physical disease to embrace myself in the flesh, I couldn't write bodiless prose," she writes. Her work, so deeply informed by her illness, has a visceral power that can only come from an embodied voice.

Cheryl Marie Wade and Nancy Mairs aren't afraid to tell the truth about their bodies and their lives. We all need to tell the truth about every aspect of our fruitflesh. It is often that which we try to avoid that can give our work the greatest power and offer the greatest healing.

Aging

ALICE AND THE GROCER

Alice looks old and distorted
in the slanted mirror above the apricots—
dried and unnaturally orange.
How could this happen? *she wonders,*
pulling at her colored hair,
pondering what's to come.
The grocer sees her pause
between the grapes and raisins.
He knows Alice is afraid of change.
Can I help you? *he asks.*
Alice doesn't think he can.
She thinks they've grown smaller
and less themselves since she last saw him.
But the grocer, rearranging the prunes,
seems hopeful. If he's kind to her,
she'll cry. He watches her walking
towards the automatic doors.
They'll let you out as easily
as they let you in, *says the bagboy,*

who'll be the grocer soon.
Alice doesn't like the bagboy.
She's thinking of the grocer's
wrinkled fingers, the thin sleeves
of his shirt. Uncertain of his name,
Alice loves the grocer—
she'd like to tell him everything.
He follows Alice to the open doors,
his arms filled with purple fruit.
Those were plums, *she says,*
moving further from the mirrors.
Yes, *says the grocer,*
who wants her not to go,
and now they're something else.

LESLEY DAUER

I know a woman who used to lead an experimental theater group in a nursing home. She observed that a person's traits often intensify as they grow older. If you are fearful when you are young, you will be even more so when you get old. If you are kind, your kindness will increase exponentially with time. This makes sense to me. A raisin's flavor is more concentrated, intense, than the young, watery sweetness of a grape. All the excess is burned away; what's left is the true essence, the true taste.

Write about the changes you've noticed—in your perception, your personality, as well as your body—as you've grown older. Catalog those changes in a loving, clear-eyed way. If you have fears about aging, acknowledge them, explore them, try to let them go.

Can you distill your own true essence from your list of changes? How would you describe your own innermost core? Be sure to observe yourself with great tenderness as you do so.

Mortality

RETROSPECT IN THE KITCHEN

After the funeral I pick
forty pounds of plums from your tree
Earth Wizard, Limb Lopper
and carry them by DC 10
three thousand miles to my kitchen

and stand at midnight—nine o'clock
your time—on the fourth day of your death
putting some raveled things
unsaid between us into the boiling pot
of cloves, cinnamon, sugar.

Love's royal color
the burst purple fruit bob up.
MAXINE KUMIN

One of the most profound things our bodies teach is the fact that we're going to die. None of us is immortal. The atoms that make up our bodies, however, are. The second law of thermodynamics tells us, "Matter can never be created or destroyed, just transformed." The atoms that make up your eyes could have been tulips five hundred years ago. Your tongue may one day be part of a manta ray. Just like leaves that fall to the ground and fertilize new growth with their mulch, we're all part of everything, in life and in death.

Our bodies, though—our current, living bodies—will not always exist. Our writing fingers will not always be fingers. When we remember this, when we carry this awareness in our bodies, it helps us live our lives more fully, with gratitude and tenderness. It helps make each moment precious, letting us be more present, in our lives and in our writing, since we know this life is not ours to keep.

How does your awareness of mortality affect you and your relationship with your body? What would you write if you only had one year to live? One day? Would you even choose to write at all? Anne Lamott shares, "I might want to write on my last day on earth, but I'd also be aware of other options that would feel at least as pressing. I would want to keep whatever I did simple, I think. And I would want to be present."

Write about what you would do if you knew it was your last day on earth. Detail where you would want to be, who you would want to be with, how you would want to fill your senses. Would you want to go out with a bang, do something you had never done before, like jumping out of an airplane? Or would you want the moment to be like breath against dandelion fluff—a soft, quiet scattering? How does it feel to document your imagined last moments?

Legacy

Whatever I do, the responsibility is mine,
but like the one who plants an orchard,
what comes of what I do, the fruit,
will be for others.
LALLA, fourteenth-century Kashmiri poet,
translated by Coleman Barks

What do you hope will survive you when you are gone? Jam from your plums? Your words on a shelf? How do you want your life to affect the world? What trace do you wish to leave in your wake?

In her wonderful poem "Take My Body," Elizabeth Weber bequeaths her bones to her daughter and tells her what to make of them—a barrette out of her left shinbone, a pen from her right forearm "detailed / with all the first words: mama, / papa, no, why, don't, bye-bye," a knife from her breastbone "to use when / / danger comes." She tells her daughter to lift her pelvic bone to her ear and listen to it as she would a shell. The poem ends with these lines: "The skull is nothing: / give it to the cat to play with."

Two artists I know have made a pact: when one of them dies, the survivor will mix some of his friend's ashes into paint and create a painting with it.

What do you want the legacy of your body to be? To whom would you bequeath your bones or ashes? What would you want to be made from them? Write a "will" that catalogs the fruits you want to leave behind once you've finished planting the orchard of your life.

Fruitflesh Meditation: Lemon

Hold a lemon up to your nose. Inhale the scent. Isn't it hard to believe something that smells so sweet could be so sour inside?

Slice the lemon open. Does the juice sting your fingers? Cut off a wedge. Bite into it. How does your face react? Do you pucker? Do you try to close yourself off from the sensation?

When bitter subjects come up as you write, don't tighten yourself against them. Don't clench your writing muscles to avoid facing the strong taste. Let the sour stuff out. If you keep it hidden under a sweet-smelling skin, it will begin to fester and rot. Release it when it is still bright and strong. Welcome its pungent bite.

PART SIX

Buds

The writer spreads the fragrance of new flowers,
an abundance of sprouting buds.
Lu Chi (261–303),
from *The Art of Writing*, translated by Sam Hamill

We can find an abundance of writing material in the most ordinary places. The small, precious buds of our everyday life can yield extraordinary stories when we grant them deep enough attention.

Fruitflesh Meditation: Kumquat

A kumquat is a budlike citrus fruit, about the size of a robin's egg. For a small fruit, it packs a real punch. Its peel tastes like an orange lollipop, but the bitter pulp inside can make you wince.

Pop a whole kumquat into your mouth. Feel its shape with your tongue. Suck some of the sweetness off the skin. Now sink your teeth in. Be prepared for a wallop of sour.

Words are small, but they can hold a lot of power. When you write, let each word be as strong and surprising as a kumquat.

Daily Life

The brilliant mango flesh divides
beneath the clean arcs of her blade.
She wants these crescent suns to fill

her bowl by noon, and so she breaks
the rhythm of her wrist just once
to wave the gathering flies away
from the heap of oval seeds.

MARISA DE LOS SANTOS, from "For Tía Josefina"

It is easy for us to sleepwalk through our everyday life. Our schedules can become so routine, so taken for granted, that we forget to pay full attention to every moment.

Choose an activity you do every day—slicing fruit for your children's lunch, brushing your teeth, washing your hair, checking the mail, feeding the goldfish—and enter it with mindfulness. Try to be aware of each movement of your body, each sensation, each flicker of thought. Enter the activity as if it were the first time; enter it as if it were a dance. See if you can discover anything new inside your regular routine when you break it down, break it open. Find a way to make it fresh on the page, in all its everyday glory.

Work

The thin neon light spills on the hands in the tubs,
the pale halves of the pears that must be dipped in salt water to
keep from turning brown,
the endless procession of cans that moves past the women
now and at midnight and dawn and on and on
even in sleep, even in dream.
Fingers turn wrinkled, turn pale like the pears,
take on a life of their own as they nestle the slippery fruit
spoonfashion in the can,
barely stopping to push the straggling hair back under the scarf.
No time to talk, no time to look up,
nothing to look up at.
Time has stopped, there is no yesterday, no tomorrow, no moment
but now, no place but here,
this slave ship hurtling through empty space.
And at the whistle which rends the rumble and clatter and din
    that
taught their ears not to hear,
the women stumble outside like children woken too early for
school,
stretching stiff limbs and creaking necks, testing a voice rusty from
lack of use.
Still dazzle-eyed, they look up and see
stars in their multitudes blazing over their heads.

Ilze Mueller

We work in our bodies. Whether we work at a fruit cannery, a law firm, a school, a mechanic's shop, a massage parlor, a farm, or a home office, our hands and eyes and lungs and brains are all engaged at certain levels.

Write about the different jobs you've had. Include all your duties, all the little physical details about the work environment, all the rhythms your body became attuned to there. Look at your job as a dance—what movements comprised it? Be as specific as possible.

Sleep

PEACHES—SIX IN A TIN BOWL, SARAJEVO

If peaches had arms
surely they would hold one another
in their peach sleep.

And if peaches had feet
it is sure they would
nudge one another
with their soft peachy feet.

And if peaches could
they would sleep
with their dimpled head
on the other's
each to each.

Like you and me.

And sleep and sleep.
SANDRA CISNEROS

Do you sleep like a peach? A tiger? A body of water?

Imagine a time-lapse camera has captured a night of your sleep. Just as you can watch clouds sweep across the sky, from sunrise to sunset, or a flower unfurl from the soil and blossom in a matter of seconds on film, watch your sleeping body move, fast-forward, through the night. Do you thrash? Slither? Do you speak, cry out? Do your eyes open, twitch, shift beneath their lids? What is your sleeping relationship with your pillow, your sheet, the person who sleeps beside you?

Imagine a vocabulary for sleep. What words, what sounds evoke sleep? What words, what sounds evoke wakefulness? How do these vocabularies differ? What can the sleeping body articulate as it shifts in and out of dream?

Write about your visualized night of sleep. How can you get beneath your own somnolent skin?

Dream Bodies

I dreamed that I floated at will in the great Ether, and I
saw this world floating also not far off, but diminished to
the size of an apple. Then an angel took it in his hand
and brought it to me and said, "This must thou eat."
And I ate the world.
RALPH WALDO EMERSON

Our dream bodies do not follow the laws of our physical bodies. Gravity, ethics, the normal boundaries of space and time hold no court here. In dreams we eat the world and the world eats us in countless astonishing ways.

How do you live in your dream body? Are you a mostly visual dreamer, or do all your senses wake up after you fall asleep? What do your dream hands touch? What does your dream tongue taste? Are your dreams candy colored, or are they washed in tones of sepia? How does your dream body respond to the environment it moves through? Are you a shape-shifter, your body morphing from one form to another, or do you feel solid as stone?

Get inside your dream skin, and see what it can tell your waking self. You can write about a specific dream, or you can evoke the general mood that suffuses your dreams. Entering our creative process is much like entering a dream; when we become more aware of our dream bodies, our dream selves, it can bring a fluid new dimension to our work.

Weather

HEAT
O wind, rend open the heat,
cut apart the heat,
rend it to tatters.

Fruit cannot drop
through this thick air—
fruit cannot fall into heat
that presses up and blunts
the points of pears
and rounds the grapes.

Cut the heat—
plough through it,
turning it on either side
of your path.
H.D. (HILDA DOOLITTLE)

Think about heat, how your body responds to it. Think about cold. Think about rain and hail and windstorms. Think about frost. Think about the many ways weather can touch us.

The weather is something everybody talks about, usually in a pedantic way. Weather can inspire some incredibly fresh, vivid writing, though. Consider the language of meteorology—cyclone and sleet, warm front and sea smoke. Consider the names for different types of clouds—cirrus, stratus, cumulus, all their various combinations, including mammatocumulus—clouds with breast-shaped protuberances on their bellies—which sound as if they should rain milk!

Go outside. Be alive to the world around you. Write about how the temperature and humidity touch your skin.

What kind of weather lives within your body? "We're here so briefly, weather / with bones," writes Wyatt Townley. Are you stormy, thunder booming in your rib cage, or is your spine filled with buttery sun? Write your body's own meteorology report.

Elements

All elements are present in a fruit tree. The tree is rooted to the earth. Those roots draw water from the soil and send it to every part of the tree's body. The leaves have a constant conversation with the air, taking in carbon monoxide, breathing out oxygen. Sunfire is present in every one of the trees cells. Each branch, each fruit holds every element beneath its skin.

We hold these elements inside our skin as well. There is water in our blood, our tears, our sweat, all our swirling fluids. There is fire in our metabolism and in the way our bodies burn with desire. Air rushes through our mouths, our lungs, filling us, spilling back out. We take the fruits of the earth into our bodies; our bodies themselves are fruits of the earth.

Write a paragraph or stanza about each of the elements inside you. Where do you find your fire? Your earth? Your water? Your air? Which element sings most loudly within your cells?

Seasons

If you go to a local farmer's market, you can find out what's truly in season—peaches in the summer, apples in the fall, quince in the winter, strawberries in the spring. At a large grocery store you can buy tomatoes—normally a summer fruit—year round. Much of the produce at big supermarkets is not grown locally; much of it is not even grown under the sun but under glass, under tents, severed from its natural growing cycle.

We often live like produce in the supermarket. Electric lights can keep us out of sync with daily rhythms; we often spend much of our time indoors, in cars, removed from the subtleties of seasonal changes. Our bodies still respond to the seasons, though. Our skin may get dry in the winter; our hair may turn curly during the spring rains; our arms may darken in the summer; our hay fever may kick up in the fall. How does your body respond to the cycles of the year? What particular scents and sights and sounds do you associate with each season? Do you have a favorite time of the year? Jot down a few notes about each season—the crunch of snow under your winter boots, the first plum of the summer, the emergence of spring lilies—then choose one season and flesh it out on the page.

Conversations with Trees

A subtle communion and communication sometimes takes place between human beings and other beings on earth. In a green twilight, we took the cut-across from Upper Cut Meat to Spring Creek, and on the flat prairie road dust rose like a signal that we were headed down into the pines. Just then, as we slowed to drive the car over ruts

and gouges, we passed a plum tree in the regalia of her
fruit. She saw me. My confusion and my need. My grief
clearer to her than to others I knew.

Years later, when I lived with Ernie in Eau Claire,
Wisconsin, I had the same feeling—a wild plum looked at
my life in its entirety. I had to stop on that autumn road
and pay attention, for the plum tree at that moment knew
my whole life.

ROBERTA J. HILL, from "Immersed in Words," in *Speaking for the Generations: Native Writers on Writing*

Plants, in their patience, their rootedness, their steady reach toward the sun, have much to teach us about how to live. We are always communicating, communing, with plants in subtle ways— we breathe in the oxygen they breathe out; they take the carbon dioxide from our lungs into their cells—but we can also make this connection more conscious and direct.

In *The Attentive Heart: Conversations with Trees*, Stephanie Kaza writes,

At some fundamental level this tree and I are made of the
same rhythms. We share a common understanding,
available in the meeting place of touch. Reaching out, I
find a simple way to begin a conversation. Coming close,
I offer my hands in greeting.

Begin a conversation, through touch, with a tree, a flower, a blade of grass. Sit in silence with this green surge of life, and see whether you are able to sense any of your common rhythms, the places where you find common ground. Think of the ways you both drink water, the ways you both drink in light. Can you find any parallels to photosynthesis within your body, your experience? What can this plant form tell you about your own life? Write about your encounter.

Light

LIME LIGHT
One can't work
by lime light.

A bowl full
right at
one's elbow

produces no
more than
a baleful
glow against
the kitchen table.

The fruit purveyor's
whole unstable
pyramid

doesn't equal
what daylight did.
KAY RYAN

Take a moment to notice the quality of light around you. Are you reading by a humming fluorescent bulb? Moonlight? Noonday sun? A bowl full of limes? Note how the light falls across these words, how it falls across your skin. Does your body cast a shadow against a wall? Is the sun sifting through leaves, tossing bright shards across your lap? Describe the flicker, the glow, of whatever illuminates your writing hands.

Think about your relationship with light. Do you get depressed in the winter months when the sun sets early, or do you need to flip shades over your eyes when the first rays hit? Is there a certain time or place that holds your favorite quality of light? Can you capture that light in words?

Try to be aware of how light moves throughout the day, how in the course of the afternoon the sun will seep from chair to floor to desk to bookshelf and then slowly fade away. Note how light alters objects in its path, transforming a blue glass into a glowing cylinder of sapphire, then turning it dull again. Choose something—a window, a candlestick, your face—and write about how it changes as the light shifts and spreads.

Darkness

The long night slips along
Fruitful, very fruitful
Spreading here, spreading there
Spreading this way, spreading that way
Propping up earth, holding up sky
The time passes, this night of Kumulipo
Still it is night
from *The Kumulipo: A Hawaiian Creation Chant*, attributed to
Keaulumoku, 1700, translated by Martha Warren Beckwith

Creation begins in darkness, the fertile, shadowy space inside our bodies. One of our greatest human fears is fear of the dark, yet the night—and our fear of it—has much to teach us. We can't mine gems in our work without traveling down some coal black shafts. As Marilyn Krysl writes, "If you deny the dark / you make a mockery of light." We need both to be whole.

Tonight, let the darkness envelop you. Notice how the dark first asserts itself. Sometimes day slips into night quietly. Try to be aware of the shifting palette of the sky, the subtle nuances that lead from light to dark. How does it feel to be in twilight? Can you find words, images, forms that can capture this gorgeous limbo state?

As night continues to fall, turn off all the lamps, and take the dusk into your skin. Be still, let your breath soften, get quiet enough so you can really feel the absence of light all around you. How does your body respond? Which of your senses become most acute? If the space is clear enough, move around a bit. (If your eyes begin to adjust themselves so you can see, close them.) Is your sense of space altered at all? Take the time to really inhabit the night, to sit with it, let it fill you. If you feel fear, don't contract against it; honor the feeling, explore it, see if you can find its roots, its dim bones. When you are ready, turn on some soft light and write about your experience, or, if you choose, you can write in the dark.

Object Lessons

When you open the wrapping (there's no card), you find a bowl, a green bowl with a white interior, a bowl for fruit or mixing. You're puzzled, but obediently put four bananas inside and then go back to whatever you were doing before: a crossword puzzle. You wonder and hope this is from a secret admirer but if so, you think, why a bowl? What are you to learn and gain from a green and white fruit bowl?
AIMEE BENDER, from "The Bowl"

We have much to learn and gain from a green and white fruit bowl—truly, from any object. We can give our writing new authenticity and precision when we take the time to describe a singular object with real clarity. Opening our senses to an object is like opening a present: we give ourselves the gift of the present moment, the gift of the object, and all it presents to us.

Pattiann Rogers was once asked how she would approach writing a poem if she had been shuttled up to a space station. She said,

> The way I would begin a poem like that would be the way
> I would begin any poem. I would start with the senses,
> and I would start with my sensual pleasure in what I
> was experiencing; or I would describe a physical object
> very carefully and then see if anything else rose out of
> that. That to me is the salvation. Salvation is in the
> physical object, whether it's my body, a locust, an egret, an
> iris, or a man-made object in space. In the particular
> object lies all that I discover.

Choose an object—a bowl, a pen, a baseball cap, whatever object calls to you from your immediate surroundings. Look at the object as if you have never set eyes upon it before; touch it as if you had never experienced such textures. Explore all its surfaces, all its detail. Write about the object; describe it as carefully as possible, using as many senses as the object will accommodate. This can be a wonderful way to train your senses, your writing, to be open and precise.

Once you've described the object, you can see if anything, as Rogers says, rises out of your description. The bowl may decide to fill itself with metaphor. It may present itself to you as a womb, an empty stomach; it may launch an essay about your mother's kitchen, a poem about the washing of hands. Let the object take you where it wants to go, but be sure you capture the thing itself first before it begins to seep over its own edges.

Clothes

He wore white shoes and a yellow sports jacket, and
Ellen could not help thinking of the yellow jackets that
hovered around the pears when her mother ate lunch in
the backyard during the summer.
NANCY WILLARD, from *Sister Water*

What are you wearing? Obscene phone callers are fond of this question, but it can be a fruitful one for a writer to ask, as well. The ways a person chooses to cloak her body can say scads about her character. When we write about people, fictional or not, it helps to know as many details about those people as possible, including what they are wearing. A woman who wears ironed jeans and red high heels is probably a very different character than a woman who is fond of Birkenstocks and billowy peasant blouses.

Do your characters sleep in peignoirs, or do they wear the same rumpled clothes for days? Clothes may cover the body, but they can reveal much about how a person lives in her body. Even when we don't describe our characters explicitly on the page, it helps us as writers if we can visualize what kind of underwear, what kind of jackets, they are wearing.

Write about what you're wearing right now or what you wore earlier in the day. How do these clothes feel against your skin? What clothes are you most at home in? What do these clothes say about you?

Photos

*We were disappointed when the pictures came back, a
whole thirty-six exposure roll of film, and only one
picture came out. It was of Ona. She's standing alone in
front of the wooden grave-marker, holding a big orange
in her hand.*

FAE MYENNE NG, from *Bone*

Find a photograph that intrigues you—one from your own
album or an antique store or a magazine. Let your writing fingers
bring the picture to life. You can choose to write from the perspec-
tive of someone in the photo, or you can be an omniscient narrator,
fleshing out the scene. Photos appeal to the visual sense alone;
bring the other senses into the frame. What smells, what textures,
what sounds are taking place? What happened just before the pic-
ture was taken? What happened right afterward? Take the two-
dimensional image off the glossy paper, and help it breathe in three
full, embodied, dimensions.

Music

*On an impulse, Constancia plucks an apple from the
bowl in the living room and lifts it to her mouth. A music
starts up in her brain, a September music, somber and
dark. Constancia drops the apple, dusts off a thick black
record, Jose Ardevol's Symphony in F-sharp, and settles
on the sofa to listen.*

CRISTINA GARCIA, from *The Agüero Sisters*

What music haunts you? Does a particular song hit you in the
solar plexus as soon as the first notes swell into the air?

Think of how a melody can conjure up a certain time of your life, can stir up vivid sensations, evoke a trancelike mood. Think of how a series of tones can alter our heartbeat, our breath, can move our bodies in innumerable ways.

Choose a song that strikes a chord inside you. Listen to it, and tune in to the different ways your body responds. Now write a piece that is informed by this song and your own response to it. You can alternate lines of the lyrics with your own words, like a call and response, or you can use a few lines as an epigraph, a place to leap from. You can name a character after a character in the song and let her tell her own story. You can weave lyrics from the song into your dialogue. Or you can simply let the song play in the background of your work, acting as soundtrack to whatever decides to unfold on the page.

Stepping-Stones

Mrs. Walker brought a persimmon to class
and cut it up
so everyone could taste
a Chinese apple. *Knowing*
it wasn't ripe or sweet, I didn't eat
but watched the other faces.

My mother said every persimmon has a sun
inside, something golden, glowing,
warm as my face.

Once, in a cellar, I found two wrapped in newspaper,
forgotten and not yet ripe.
I took them and set both on my bedroom windowsill,
where each morning a cardinal
sang, The sun, the sun.
LI-YOUNG LEE, from "Persimmons"

When an object is familiar to us, it can act like a stepping-stone in our memory, appearing again and again across our path, allowing us to take leaps from one part of our life to another.

Persimmons become stepping-stones for Li-Young Lee in his poem. As the full poem unfolds, the fruit leads him to his sixth grade classroom, his childhood bedroom; it gives him an opening to explore his challenges with language, his early sexuality, his father's blindness. The persimmon holds more than sugary pulp for Lee; it is rife, ripe, with memory and association, "heavy as sadness / and sweet as love."

Choose an object—an apple, a T-shirt, a teacup—something you have had a fair amount of physical contact with. It can be a singular object, such as one particular teacup, or a class of objects—all the teacups you have raised to your lips. Write about three specific instances in which you interacted with this object. Where were you? Who were you with? What sensations, what emotions did the object stir up for you? Flesh out each memory as much as possible. Now find a way to thread these memories together. You may be surprised by the wild associations, the previously unknown paths you are able to unearth.

Crowds

The aisle is jammed, strangers touching the length of their bodies,
ignoring each other, families bored with this closeness. I think of
the white slivers inside banana flowers, all lined up waiting to
burst into hands of fruit. I smile at the women, wink at the
children, look at the men with the best openhearted sexually
blank look I can muster, walking the line between here and there,
all the verbs for "going" conjugated ineptly, so many rules, and
the only one posted is No Riding Wet.
BARBARA RÀS, from "The Bus That Travels Only by Day"

How do you experience being in a crowd, being one body in
a sea of bodies? Do you find it freeing? Claustrophobic? Write a
detailed crowd scene that captures all the life that swirls around
you, all the sensations and impressions you experience in the thrall
of the throng. The elbows that jostle you, the smells of other people's
bodies—sweat and perfume and garlicky breath; the way people
keep stepping on the back of your shoes; the snippets of conversa-
tion that drift into your ear; the pink hat of the woman a few yards
ahead that sails above the horde like a boat.

Have you ever momentarily lost your parent or child or friend
in a swarm of people? Write about that feverish, panicky, disoriented
feeling; write about how it felt when you found each other again.

Virtual Travel

. . . there are the soft syllabic fruits of Brazil
yet to taste . . .
KATHLEEN FRASER, from "Because You Aren't Here
to Be What I Can't Think Of"

Writing is like a passport. It can take us anywhere we want to go, and it's much cheaper than a plane ticket!

Where do you want to go? You can research this place to imbue your fantasy with authentic detail, or you can just let your imagination guide you on your journey as you write. You can even invent an entirely new location, à la Willy Wonka's Chocolate Factory or Digitopolis from *The Phantom Tollbooth*. Fully imagine yourself at your destination; what does the air smell like? What did you eat for lunch? What music do you hear, what language wafts all around you? How do you interact with the people who live there? Bring your whole body to the experience. Later, if you want, you can share your "vacation slides" with a friend by reading this account of your virtual travels!

Cheap Thrills

When a cherry falls off a tree, does it enjoy the rush of air, the rush of sensation before it hits the ground? Is it an exhilarating plummet?

Most likely not, but who knows?

What is the most intense thrill your body has ever experienced? A roller-coaster drop? Skydiving? A downhill bike ride?

Seeing a brilliant sunset? Having your nipple sucked just so? How does your body register that kind of rush?

Write about a thrill, be it cheap or deep. Let your words be charged with the experience so that when someone reads it, they can feel their own spine (or other parts) tingle. The right verb can capture sensation and movement beautifully. When you use a zinger of a verb, the reader can zoom and plunge and swoop and throb right along with you. Don't be afraid to make up your own verbs if you can't find one that echoes the action, the mood, you are trying to convey. Remember how the main character in the *Eloise* picture books "skibbles" around?

Fruitflesh Meditation: Quince

The quince's rich, musky scent holds delicious promise, but when you bite into the yellow fruit, the flesh is dry and tastes of wood. Do not give up. A quince takes some patience, some coddling. When cooked, the quince's flavor deepens, sweetens, becomes as haunting as its fragrance.

Peel, core, and slice a quince. Taste a bit raw. Can you tell it's not quite ready to be consumed? Put the quince in a pot with enough apple juice or wine or sugar water to cover. Cover the pot and simmer until tender, about half an hour. Now taste the fruit. See how it has come into its own?

Be patient with yourself as you write. Sometimes your words may seem tough and tasteless when they first come into the world, despite their brilliant early promise. Let them simmer a bit longer. Give them time to mellow, soften, sweeten before you taste them again.

PART SEVEN

Flowers

And the day came when the risk to remain tight in the bud
was more painful than the risk it took to blossom.

ANAÏS NIN

When the time comes to take your writing to the next level, leap fearlessly. Experiment with form, learn as much as you can about craft, figure out how to shape and polish your raw material into something that glows. Risk blossoming, both on the page and off.

Fruitflesh Meditation: Tomato

The tomato is a misunderstood fruit. Many people think it's a vegetable. Centuries ago, it was considered poisonous. For a while, it was mistaken for an aphrodisiac. As is the case with many misunderstood artists, though, the tomato eventually came to be appreciated for its true, natural genius.

Slice a tomato. Gaze at the red luster of the skin, the glistening seeds inside. No matter how misunderstood the tomato ever was, it kept going, kept growing. It knew it was delicious even when no one else did.

Take a bite of the tomato. Let the integrity of its rich, tangy flavor fill you up. Explore the different layers of texture—the slick surface surrounding the seeds, the glossy skin that snaps between your teeth, the sometimes granular, sometimes silky inner flesh. Note how complex fruit can be beneath its smooth, round surface.

Many writers have felt misunderstood at some crucial juncture in their lives. Writing is often a response to that. It is a way for a person to assert her fruitfulness when the world tries to convince her she's a vegetable.

Stay true to your writing, whether or not others understand what you're doing. You know the power of your own seeds. You know the truth of your own fruitflesh. Someone, eventually, will come to appreciate your most singular flavor.

Ripening

As for my next book, I am going to hold myself from
writing it till I have it impending in me: grown heavy in
my mind like a ripe pear; pendant, gravid, asking to be
cut or it will fall.

Virginia Woolf, quoted in *Writers on Writing*

Each story, each poem, has its own gestation period. Some
stories need to ripen inside for years before they are ready to push
their way into the world. Others burst forth at the slightest provo-
cation; an image, a single word, can sometimes set the ball(point)
rolling. Most pieces of writing will tell you what they require—
whether they need to tiptoe carefully down the path or grab you by
the hair and pull you along for the ride. Each story or poem grows
pendant, gravid, at its own organic pace. Sometimes we need to gen-
tly prod it—and ourselves—forward if things begin to stagnate, but
for the most part the writing will determine its own momentum.

Writers as well often have their own innate modus operandi.
Some writers prefer to map out every step of the journey, using out-
lines, note cards, detailed character histories to act as signposts
along the way toward the finished story. Others prefer to let the
work unfold organically, following it down one surprising road after
another. Neither path is "right"; what's important is that you find
the process that feels right for *you*.

If you are new to writing, or haven't yet discovered your
most productive mode, play around with different approaches.
Construct a detailed outline of something you want to write, and
see how it feels to flesh it out. Then, sometime later, choose a
word from your outline, freewrite about it for ten minutes, and see
what emerges. Which process feels more comfortable to you, more
like home? Many writers use a combination of the two, switching
back and forth between them, depending upon what the story
calls for.

Everyone's creative process is unique. Some writers need to sit down at their desk for a prescribed number of hours each day; others write only when the spirit moves them. Some worry they'll give the energy of their writing away if they talk about it; others are energized by discussing works in progress. Keep experimenting until you discover your own juiciest patterns of ripening.

Now I Know My ABCs . . .

When Number 127 is being asked to spell LOQUAT,
Eliza closes her eyes and feels her mind empty out. L fills
her head, a glowing yellow the color of molten metal. . . .
Inside Elly's head, L grows longer, its edges curving
inward to form an O. Her body loosens. When the edge of
O grows a tail to become Q, Eliza feels the change in her
fingertips. Q's top evaporates and its tail disappears, U
settling warm in her belly. Elly feels a tickle as U flips and
grows a line through its middle to become an A. When A's
legs slide together as its arm floats up, T fills Eliza,
straightening her spine. Eliza opens her eyes. She feels as
if she has just woken from a deep sleep. Number 127 is
walking offstage to the sound of vigorous applause.
Myla Goldberg, from *Bee Season*

Writers often have an intense, sensual relationship with the alphabet. From the time he was a child, Vladimir Nabokov associated each letter with a "color sensation." *P* was an "unripe apple," while *H* was a "drab shoelace." *M* evoked "a fold of pink flannel," *R* a "sooty rag being ripped"; *N* felt like "oatmeal," *Z* a "thundercloud." Do you have any sensory associations with the letters of the alphabet? Do different letters live in your body in different ways—*U* humming in your throat, *T* knocking around your kneecaps?

Sing the alphabet song at different speeds, in different voices. Which letters feel good in your mouth? Write down the twenty-six letters. Which ones are a pleasure to form? Which do you find troublesome? Take the time to reacquaint yourself with the alphabet; get to know each letter again, as if for the first time. Letters are like the atoms of our language—we combine them and recombine them to create molecules of words, bodies of sentences—and it can only help our writing to get to know them more intimately. Do a "character study" of each one: does *Q* taste like asparagus? Does *G* make your feet itch? Does a cursive *S* remind you of a stand-up bass, solid and voluptuous, while a printed *S* hisses and thrashes like a garter snake? Flesh out the letters; bring them to life. When you write, let them share the journey with you, filling each word with their own colorful, quirky breath.

Metaphor

When I was a child, I remember, I walked to school on a particular path each day. On that path was a plum tree. One day I stood gazing at the plum tree, and it seemed to me that the plums looked like bats. When I pointed this out to my classmates, they were horrified—not of the plum bats but of me. They thought I was weird. Nowadays, teachers encourage children to be creative, but in my day, children were made to be as average as possible, which made it hard for creative kids like me. Anyway, that was my first metaphor.
DIANE ACKERMAN, interviewed in *The Scoop*

One of the most powerful tools in a writer's bag of tricks, metaphors bring an element of surprise, a sense of "aha!" to a sentence. They help the reader (and the writer herself!) see things in a completely fresh way. When we make connections between things that had never been connected before—like bats and plums—we most likely burn new pathways in our brain; at the very least, we open ourselves up to new, wild realms of possibility.

Writing metaphors requires an openness, a fluidity of perception. The boundary between self and other blurs when we link mouth with coin purse or swimming pool, belly button with snail or straw mushroom.

Poet Peggy Hong often plays "the metaphor game" when she is driving with her kids. She'll point out a lamppost or a window box and ask them to come up with a metaphor for it—"the lamppost is a bellhop waiting to take your luggage" or "the window box is an angry volcano ready to spew flowers."

Look at things around you right now—a phone, a pencil, a box of envelopes—and write a metaphor for each one. Let yourself go wild. Try creating associations that make no rational sense to begin with ("a phone is an elephant"), and then see if you can find a way to make this a meaningful link. ("A phone is an elephant; it has a great memory. It holds many numbers in its pachyderm brain. Its trunk scoops watery voices into my ear. . . .")

Contact Lenses

I want to see with Mary's eyes:
how the cattails turn to ermine
then shed their white fur.

How the blackberries, nearly ripe,
hang from brambles like garnet earrings.
Linda Neal Reising, from "Mary's Eyes" (to Mary Oliver)

Sometimes we can see the world more clearly through another author's eyes. Sometimes another writer's voice can help us find our own.

Think of a writer you love, a writer whose work offers a shimmering example of what you think good writing can be. Choose a sample of that writer's work, and write it out in your own hand. This is not plagiarism; you won't claim this work as your own. It's simply a way for you to take that writer's language into your own body. See how it feels to shape those words with your own fingers, your own wrists. See how possible it is for your own body to produce such beauty.

Read the work of one of your favorite writers out loud. The writer's breath becomes your breath. The words that formed in the writer's throat find their way into your own mouth. You can feel the rhythm of the language that much more intimately when you give it voice, when you lay your voice on top of the author's, like a two-part harmony.

You can enter a dialogue with this writer, either on the page or spoken aloud. After each line of the poem, or each sentence of the story, create a line or sentence of your own in response. Don't worry about making sense. Just find a way to let your own work resonate with your beloved writer's, line by line, breath by breath.

You can also choose to translate the writer's poem or story into your own tongue. What is the essence of the piece? Choose one line, one sentence, that seems to capture the spirit of the work, and use it as a springboard for your own poetry or prose, your own essential expression. When you do this, your contact with the writer's work becomes a lens—a contact lens that helps clarify your own vision.

Wolffia Globosa

In the course of writing this book, I discovered that the smallest fruit in the world is tinier than a grain of salt and grows on a rootless aquatic plant that belongs to the duckweed family. Even though I doubt I will ever see one of these microscopic, bladderlike fruits in real life, I am enriched by knowing they exist in the world. Plus, strange facts do have a way of seeping into my work; I have a feeling one day the *Wolffia globosa* will decide to insert its tiny body into one of my poems or stories.

We are often told to write what we know. This is good advice; when we "know" something deeply, intimately, the writing that comes from it will be rich and vibrant, full of authentic detail. We don't always have to experience something directly to understand it with our fruitflesh, however; there are many different ways of "knowing." Our bodies have great imaginations.

Research is one way we can extend the scope of our own knowledge. Pattiann Rogers writes, "Although research has played a part in the writing of many of my poems, some have come into being *solely* because of research. I find that most research, even the slightest, opens doors of thought for me and offers new, evocative, and interesting vocabulary."

Think of a subject that interests you. Find out as much as you can about this subject. Do a search on the Internet, thumb through the encyclopedia, check out what the library has to offer, see if there is an expert in your area you can talk to or maybe even a hands-on activity that would help you gain a deeper knowledge of the subject. Whether you're looking into the mating habits of jellyfish or the history of masonry or the inner workings of a bearded iris, find facts and details that resonate with you, that excite you in some way.

Once you feel you have gathered enough research, find a way to incorporate the information into writing that is personal and artful. Don't write a dry book report; don't just regurgitate the facts.

Find a way to connect your body, your life, to the things you discovered. Can you find parallels between the jellyfish's habits and your own sexuality? Can you weave connections between the blossoming of the iris and your own creative unfolding? Research can provide us with a more expansive capacity for metaphor, a richer well of material for us to draw from. It can help our senses embrace the most distant star as well as the tiniest fruit on the planet.

Etymology

When Eliza studies, she travels through space and time. In COUSCOUS, she can sense desert and sand-smoothed stone. In CYPRESS, she tastes salt and wind. She visits Africa, Greece, and France. Each word has a story: a Viking birth, a journey across the sea, the exchange from mouth to mouth, from border to border, until œpli is apfel is appel is APPLE, crisp and sweet on Eliza's tongue. When it is night and their studying complete, these are the words she rides into sleep. The voice of the dictionary is the voice of her dreams.
MYLA GOLDBERG, from *Bee Season*

The dictionary can teach us so much more than the meaning of a word. It can also teach us the rich root of that word, its evolution, its history. It is good for us to trace words back to their birth, to get a taste of their origins; it can only help us as writers if we get to know our language more intimately.

Choose a word you love, and search for its beginnings. What can you learn about the word by discovering its roots? If you can't find the real story, make one up. Words pass through many mouths and hands, burnished to a sheen, before they find their way to us.

Write about the journey of one of these words. How did it travel from the tongue that first uttered it in Mesopotamia all the way to your computer keyboard? Does the flavor of its origins still linger on your lips?

Some words have a shiny root embedded inside of them. *Chant*, for example, is the root of *enchantment*. Play Boggle with a word, and see how many other words are breathing under its skin. Can you make a poem, a sentence, out of the words you find? Going back to *enchantment*, we can pull out, among many other possibilities: *teach me that tame heat* and *chant, mean hen*. Words hold many surprises inside the clean lines of their letters; it is up to us to tease them out.

Writer's Block

Boughs, too, drooped low above him, big with fruit,
Pear trees, pomegranates, brilliant apples,
Luscious figs, and olives, ripe and dark;
But if he stretched his hand for one, the wind
Under the dark sky tossed the bough beyond him.
HOMER, from *The Odyssey*

If there is a better description of writer's block than Homer's depiction of Tantalus in Hades, I don't know of it. When we are blocked, the promise of our own creative fruitfulness hangs—*tantalizingly*, one could say—before us. When we reach to grasp, it dissolves into thin air.

Fortunately, we are not ruled by the God of the Underworld. We are not damned to reach with empty hands for all eternity (although sometimes, in the throes of major writer's block, it may feel that way). We have the power to break through our blocks and grab hold of that fruit. We have the power to devour it whole.

In an interview, Isabel Allende once said, "One gets blocked, very often, because an artist, for example, can only relate to the world through his eyes, or a writer through his writing. They lose the capacity for playfulness with the other senses, and that blocks them."

If you are feeling blocked, step away from your writing. Open your senses. Lose yourself in color. Smell five different flowers. Eat a mystery fruit. Find seven different textures. Listen to music or rushing water. Dance.

Jean Houston once wrote about how she dances when she has writer's block. At first she dances for the simple joy of dancing, to get her blood pumping good and hard. Then she dances the subject she is writing about.

Try this: if you are writing fiction and get blocked, dance the way your characters would dance, each one in turn. It will give you a deeper insight into how they live in their bodies. If you are writing poetry or nonfiction, transform your subject into movement; dance, and let the language boil up from your belly, swirl into your shoulders, course down your arms and through your fingers, until you can finally release it, embodied, onto the page.

If you can't get up and dance when you're blocked, write a dictionary poem or just look up some new words in the dictionary to get a fresh appreciation of language. Write nonsense. Play around with sounds. Shake up your rational mind until the blocks break loose, until your fingers can close around the fruit that hangs before your hungry eyes.

Dance Lessons

Stir a teaspoon of baking soda into a glass of lemonade, then plunk in four blueberries. Watch the fruit pop around throughout the drink. What can we do to help our words leap like this, effervescent, across the page?

In beginning dance classes, teachers often introduce their students to the different qualities of movement: sustained, percussive, lyrical, chaotic, and still. Each of our movements is rooted in at least one of these qualities, in life as well as the ballet studio. We can apply their rhythms to our writing, as well, especially if we take them into our bodies first. Forget about appearances as you do these sustained and percussive exercises. Close your eyes, and let yourself go crazy. Concentrate on how the movements feel inside your body, not how they look.

Sustained movement is looong, slooow, stretched out like taffy. Tai chi is a good example of this, the movement gorgeously drawn out and smooth. Try moving in a sustained way—preferably with your whole body, but even just your arm will do. Let your wrist and elbow undulate like a snake; let your ribs do a slow, sexy figure eight. Feel the way your body carves the air; feel each slow and sinuous shift of muscle. Can you write a sentence, a paragraph, that sustains this sustained movement? Are there any sounds—soft vowels, liquid consonants—that could help contribute to this luscious lingering sense? Pick up a pen, and move it in a sustained way across the paper. You may want to start with just shapes, curves, and swoops of ink, and see if those lines choose to melt into words.

Percussive movement is the opposite of sustained. It is sharp. Quick. Stac-ca-to. Let yourself move in a percussive way— jerk your head back and forth, move your arms like a robot, let your hips twitch from side to side. How can you bring this short, direct energy to your writing? Short sentences? One syl-la-ble words? Strange. Punc. Tu. A. Tion? Lots of *k*s and *t*s—sounds that cut the breath? What subjects would be especially appropriate to explore with percussive language? Move your pen percussively across the paper—just shapes first, like above; then see what words choose to fill the sharp, short space.

Alternate between the two qualities; see how their energies play off each other. As writers, we need to follow the beat of our own drummer; these exercises can help us expand our internal repertoire.

Chaos, Stillness, and Grace

the moment i entered the room, i knew i had interrupted
    something.
all was still, but it was a stillness that only comes after frantic
movement. a sensual orgy of apples, peaches and pears had been
occurring in the fruit-bowl.
BETH BEASLEY, from "fruit"

Frantic movement, sensual orgy movement, is often steeped in chaos.

ChaosIsAllOverThePlaceItIsALettingGoOfControlOfOrderOfInhi bitionItIsADroppingIntoWildness. Dance a chaos dance—let yourself go crazy, let your movements be untethered, untamed. How can you unleash this same wild energy on the page? Grab a pen and unleash the words. Scatter them over the paper, willy-nilly, pell-mell. Make some of them big, some of them small. Don't pay any attention to lines or margins—be messy, be loose, be fierce!

After chaos, it is good to drop into stillness to find some solid ground. Stillness is as crucial to movement as silence is to language. Alternate one of the other movement qualities with stillness. Feel how the stillness is inhabited—by your breath, your heartbeat. Feel how this stillness can center you in the midst of chaos, how it offers an island of peace in any sea of movement. How does stillness appear in your writing? As white space? As needed breath stops, through line breaks or punctuation? How can you consciously use stillness in your work?

Try this: write one word, then sit with that word quietly for the span of a few breaths. See what word emerges next out of the silence. Now sit in stillness with those two words until the next word chooses to present itself. Be aware of the wholeness of each word, the integrity that surrounds it. Once you have a few words, another energy quality may assert itself; you may begin to write in a sustained way, perhaps, or lyrical, or you may want to continue in stillness for a while longer. Let the work find its own internal rhythm.

Lyrical movement can contain any of the qualities we've already explored, but it ties them together with a current of grace, of beauty. This doesn't necessarily mean a narrative thread runs through it, but, like in any good plot, there is a sense of continuity, of flow. It often echoes the movements of nature—of river and wing and petal. Lyrical doesn't mean sentimental; it is the supple, strong embodiment of grace. Put on some music that sings beauty to you, and let yourself match that beauty with your movements. Don't strive to look like a prima ballerina. This is *felt* beauty, not visual beauty, you want to create for yourself. How can you imbue your words with this same lyrical power?

Most people find they are more comfortable with certain qualities than others, both in movement and in writing. It's often especially fruitful to play with the ones we don't feel as at home within. Experiment with shifting in and out between chaos and sustained movement, percussive language and stillness. Open yourself to their rhythms, and your work will find new ways to dance.

Repetition

The sentence repeating itself in your ear
as a pear repeats itself, each time a little altered,
on every branch of the tree.
JANE HIRSHFIELD, from "Great Powers Once Raged
Through Your Body"

Our bodies love repetition. Our hearts, our lungs beat out a constant rhythm—ta *tum*, ta *tum*, ta *tum*. When we come upon a repeated pulse on the page, our bodies nod in recognition. Depending on how it's used, this can lull us into a trance or give us a beat to dance to; it provides a bass note for the work, allowing the words on top of it to sing.

Many poetic forms, such as the villanelle and the sestina, are propelled by repetition, but prose writers as well can use it to great effect. In an interview, Arundhati Roy, author of *The God of Small Things*, said, "Repetition I love, and used because it made me feel safe. Repeated words and phrases have a rocking feeling, like a lullaby. They help take away the shock of the plot."

Repetition is not the same as repetitiveness, using the same words, the same ideas, over and over until they lose their freshness, become stale. Repetitiveness is often unintentional; repetition, on the other hand, is usually a conscious choice. It can provide a touchstone, a place where the reader can take a breath and say, "Okay, I know where I am." The writer can then play with reader expectation, catching the reader off guard by altering the repeated phrase. If you begin the first five paragraphs of a story with the sentence "My stomach is an aviary" and then start the sixth paragraph with "My stomach is a bestiary," the reader will know something significant has changed.

Choose a sentence or phrase that feels resonant to you—one that you make up or one from another writer. Find a way to weave this phrase into your work, whether you begin each stanza of a poem with it or throw it into every other paragraph. You can alter the phrase a little each time or not, depending on the effect you want to go for. When you are done writing, read your work aloud. How does your body respond to its heartbeat?

There Is an Apple with Me

Mae gen i afal, what we would translate into English as "I have an apple," literally means "There is an apple with me" in Welsh. In Celtic languages there is little concept of ownership, of "having" things. Things are not possessed by you; they are "with" you.

Imagine the shift in consciousness that would occur if our language suddenly didn't support the possessive case. I am with this house. I am with this car. This writing is with me. Such phrasing gives us a better sense of our place in the scheme of things. We are not the lords of the manor; we are in constant, equal interchange with the world around us. We share the world with apples and cars and one another. When we say "I am with this" rather than "This is mine," we acknowledge and respect the integrity of each individual object and being and put our relationship with it on level ground.

Write a paragraph about yourself and the things that surround you without using any possessive terms—*my, mine,* and so forth. Because of the way our language (the language that is *with* us) has developed, it would be hard to sustain this kind of writing for any length of time, but see what happens to your own perception when you try to write in a nonpossessive way.

Rots Juice Choice

We can find parallels to writing in the most unexpected places.

I recently accompanied my daughter's class on a field trip to a citrus packing plant. As we wandered around the large warehouse, watching the fruit's journey from off-the-tree wildness to polished, packaged product, I felt like I was witnessing the editing process in action.

The fruit comes into the plant raw, shaggy, organic, just the way a story or poem or essay first arrives, newborn, onto the page. The oranges then roll down a conveyor belt where they are rinsed off. This seemed to me to be like the cooling-off period, the rinsing-off period, we need away from our work before we can look at it with clear eyes. We can do superficial cleanup work on our writing during this time, straightening up a few stray words here and there, but the true editing process hasn't begun quite yet.

The wet oranges roll along more conveyor belts until they come to the sorting area. A group of women there sit on stools, carefully watching the tumbling fruit. Three chutes open before each of them, the holes marked Rots, Juice, Choice. With gloved hands, the women sort the oranges: the ones with deep and obvious flaws go into the Rots hole; the ones with cosmetic blemishes but sound bodies are sent down the Juice chute; the perfect ones are deemed Choice and go on to be packaged and shipped off to stores.

I think of these categories often as I edit my work now. I find words, sentences, paragraphs that are absolutely rotten. Those I strike immediately. Often, I find sections of work where the ideas are worth expressing but the writing itself doesn't sing; those sections I juice in order to get the essence out but in a more palatable form. Then there are the choice bits, the always surprising parts that come out whole and delicious and beg to be left in their natural state.

The packing plant not only reminded me of the personal editing process; it also made me think of the publishing process, at large. The oranges pass through many hands, many stations, before they reach their final destination. Our own work has to pass through many hands—from our own to submissions editors', assistant editors', managing editors', marketing people's, typesetters', book binders'—before it finally reaches the reader. When I hold something in my hand, be it an orange or a book or anything else that has been multiply processed, I try to remember to take a moment to acknowledge where it came from. I like to send a little subliminal message of thanks to all the people who work so hard to bring these things to my table, not to mention the trees, which provide both the fruit and the paper, and the earth, which supports all of it.

Cross-Pollination

I was pulled into "The Garden"
by your great detail, but I want more
about the onion's layers—
they moved me to tears. The energy

starts in the second stanza,
although bananas are too predictable
and I'd pare down your limes.

Could you begin the poem here:
Gathering sun-warmed blackberries in summer's
          basket . . . ?
I don't know where you are going
with the three cling peaches.
YVONNE CANNON, from "Into 'The Garden'"

"Into 'The Garden'" offers a great tongue-in-cheek dissection of what it's like to get feedback on a piece of writing. Critiques from others can be incredibly helpful. We often have a hard time looking at our own work with clarity, and an objective pair of eyes can help point out weaknesses in our writing that we ourselves cannot see. At the same time, we need to trust our own instincts; perhaps the "The Garden" poet really loves the mystery of those three cling peaches and has no desire to clarify their presence. We have to discover what amount of interaction works best for us and our work.

We can look to fruit trees to help figure out our own process. Some fruit trees are self-fertile. They do not require cross-pollination from other flowers. They can grow fruit in isolation, no special accommodations necessary. Other fruit trees are self-sterile. They can bear fruit only if dusted with pollen from another tree. Many fruit trees lie somewhere in between. They are able to bear fruit on their own, but the fruit grows more abundantly if their flowers are cross-pollinated.

What kind of a writer are you? Do you require isolation to write, with no external input? Do you need constant feedback from others? Do you flourish in a balance between the two?

When someone does offer a critique, check your gut reaction. If you feel a resonance with the advice offered, it is probably worth listening to. If you feel yourself contract against it, pay heed to this as well. Trust your own impulses. Don't give your own power or vision away. Trying someone's suggestions, however, even if they make you bristle, can never hurt. It may even help you break through your own self-imposed boundaries in a way you may never have accomplished on your own. If the changes don't feel right, you can always go back to your original version of the work.

While it may ultimately be beneficial to follow unwanted advice, it is best to stay away from people who constantly put down your work, who constantly criticize without offering any encouragement. Successful pollination can take place only between flowers of the same kind of fruit. A plum tree cannot pollinate a tangerine tree. Similarly, it's important to find people you feel some sort of affinity with—not necessarily people who are similar to you or write similar work to your own, but people who you trust and respect—when you're ready to share your writing. If you can find people who understand your work but are honest about what it needs in order to grow, you can expect some very fruitful cross-pollination.

Pruning

When I was a freshman at the University of Redlands, I took a wonderful class called "The Eye and Voice of Poetry," taught by Ralph Angel. When Ralph said *poem*, it sounded like *pomme*, or apple, something sweet and juicy in his mouth. I loved to hear him say it.

This was one of the poems I workshopped that semester:

NASHI

From Japan, my friend writes
of nashi: "It's a combo—apple
and pear—full of liquid, sweet
and crisp, but juicier than the winter
pear." His host mother had just given
him some, peeled and sliced. The juice
was still on his fingers.

I almost scream for want of nashi.

Even words about fruit make me
feel . . . the dark inner flesh
of a cherry, sultry mango, sweating
melon . . . all moist and dense,
lusty. If I could, I would eat

all of William Carlos Williams'
plums, and only ask the forgiveness
of the sweet, cold fruit.

In an earlier version of the poem, I had written "Even words about fruit make me / feel sensuous." Ralph encouraged me to cut out that last word. I resisted the change at first but came to see his point: you prune the branches of the fruit tree in order to make the tree stronger. *Sensuous* was extraneous, redundant. It didn't contribute to the health of the poem. A poem should be like a fruit—shapely, whole in itself. An extra word is like an extra stem, pulp bulging through the rind; it takes away from the integrity of the whole.

Poems are like fruit, too, in the way they need to ripen. Sometimes a poem is plucked too fast. It has not yet reached its peak of flavor; it is hard, almost tasteless. That's when you have to tuck it away in a mental paper bag like an unripe peach, let it soften, sweeten, release its fragrance. You can almost smell when it's ready to be revisited, revised, devoured.

Praise

Bananas are like poets: they only want to be told how great they are.
ERICA JONG, from "Fruits and Vegetables"

Harsh criticism can harm our creative process, but so can a reliance upon praise. Praise is nice, of course. It feels good to get a positive response to our work. That ego stroking shouldn't be why you write, though. If you become dependent on praise, your creative flow gets displaced. You become removed from your own source.

Think of a banana. A banana may get all the accolades in the world for having the brightest, glossiest skin. When you peel it open, though, that banana may very well be rotten or tasteless inside. As long as you stay grounded in your own fruitflesh, you won't be in danger of rotting away from a high-sugar, empty-calorie diet of applause. Fame is fleeting. Your creative center, on the other hand, continually refreshes itself.

Write for your own pleasure, your own unfolding, your own need to get a story out. The creative process can hold all the glory you'll ever need.

Ask yourself why you write. Let your answer guide you.

Sweet and Sour Grapes

Most of us know the story of the fox and the grapes. The poor creature tried and tried to grab some succulent fruit from a vine, but (as with Tantalus) it always dangled just out of his reach. He finally gave up, muttering that the grapes were probably sour, anyway.

What grapes do you reach for as a writer? For centuries, women writers couldn't allow themselves to be ambitious; their work was not taken seriously, much less given the respect or accord it deserved. The grapes are thankfully now within our reach. If you want to work toward literary success, go for it! Own your ambition, let it fill you with its driving energy. Never feel guilty about wanting to make your own mark on the world.

Once you set sight on your goal, though, don't forget to enjoy the rich journey along the way. When we love what we're doing, when we are fully engaged in our own creative unfolding, sour grapes never enter the picture.

What are your wildest ambitions for yourself and your writing career? Be honest with yourself. Have you already started to write your Nobel acceptance speech? Do you picture your name on the list of Pulitzer nominees? Visualize your book as an Oprah pick? Be extravagant with your fantasies. It never hurts to dream big, as long as you can keep a sense of humor about the outcome.

Taking a Break

For I have had too much
Of apple-picking: I am overtired
Of the great harvest I myself desired.
ROBERT FROST, from "After Apple Picking"

It's okay to get tired of writing. Give yourself a break when your body tells you to. Most writing teachers talk about the importance of writing every day, keeping yourself on a tight schedule. You won't hurt yourself or your work, though, if you take a day or two (or even much more) off. We all have seasons of fruitfulness and fallowness. We need time to move away from words so that when we are ready to write again, we'll have rich experiences to draw from.

Breaking from schedule is good, anyway. When couples are trying to have a baby, they often talk about how sex becomes mechanical, by the numbers, rather than a real expression of love and desire. It becomes more about the product than the process. The same thing can happen with writing. Don't just keep your eyes on the prize and lose sight of your own creative impulses. Step away from your writing if you feel tired or resistant or if you feel like you have been revising your writing to death. It is possible, after all, to overprune, to cut the vitality right out of our work. Sometimes it's crucial to step away so we can come back to it later with fresh eyes, a refreshed heart. If you need to take a break, don't write again until you feel moved to. Let yourself be wordless for a while. When the words are ready to flow, they will. Trust in that.

Fruitflesh Meditation: Star Fruit

The star fruit, or carambola, is elliptical. It splays out in five wings when whole. When you slice it, stars fall off your knife.

The skin of the star fruit is very thin. The flesh inside is translucent; it almost isn't there. The fragrance, the flavor sing out bright and clear through its luminous almost-absence.

Writing is a wonderful way to explore the self, but it is also a great way to let go of the self. When we let our egos step aside, we clear the path for pure creative energy to pass through us without getting snagged on our vanity, our defenses. We become open channels for swift currents of language, streams our egos would never dare to let us enter.

Take a star slice onto your tongue. Close your eyes. Make yourself invisible. Sometimes a writer has to become transparent in order to let the words sing through.

PART EIGHT

Fruit

*. . . to let the tongue sing each fruit,
its savor, its aroma and its use.*

Marge Piercy,
from "The art of blessing the day"

Sing each fruit of your body, each sweet swell and curve. Sing the fruitfulness of women's bodies, the ripe and juicy flesh that brings us pleasure, births new life.

Fruitflesh Meditation: Pomegranate

My father-in-law's wife, Eula, recently gave me a wonderful book, *Cooking Like a Goddess*, by Cait Johnson. In it, I was thrilled to discover, Johnson offers her own fruit meditation. I'll include most of it here:

> Pomegranates are magical fruits, not only because of their link with Persephone and her annual stay in the underworld, but because of even older associations with the womb, the sacred chalice of life. . . . Red and a little lumpy, its globular shape is certainly womblike. Its waxy smooth skin, when dried, will become tough and leathery. It has a jagged crown at its top, filled with tiny golden, strawlike fibers with round-tipped heads.
>
> With a sharp knife, cut a vulva-shape gently through the surface of your pomegranate's skin—a curved diamond-shape with tips pointing up and down. Carefully peel off the skin inside this shape. The inner skin is yellowish white; it clings to the seeds like a caul around a newborn baby. When the inner skin is peeled away, the vivid seeds are exposed. Take time to appreciate the beauty of this female symbol which you have uncovered and which the pomegranate embodies. Really look at the seeds: notice their translucence, their garnet color (the word garnet *comes from the word* granatum, *the Latin word for pomegranate). If you cut one, it bleeds. It has a subtle scent. How would you describe it?*

*Now pry one seed gently from its socket and taste it.
(In just this way did Persephone taste her first seed in
Hades.) Its outer flesh is cool and sweet, but the inner
seed is hard and bitter. It is certainly both sweet and
bitter to be a woman in our culture today. It is sweet and
bitter to be a daughter. In what other ways can you
describe the lesson of the seeds for yourself? If you count
out five more seeds and eat them, think of them as your
tickets to the inner world, the deep, underground wisdom
that the outer world of frantic busyness often makes
us forget. You have become a Persephone in your choice
to go deeper.*

In writing, we also become Persephones, each of us exploring our own fertile darkness, bringing it to light with our words. Each seed is a rich story we carry inside, waiting to spill its lasting color.

Apple Selling

In the late 1800s, a series of popular racy postcards featured women, topless, holding trays of fruit, their breasts mixed in among the apples or oranges. "Buy my apples?" the captions coyly read beneath.

As writers and women, we need to move away from viewing our fruitflesh as a marketable commodity. Instead of regarding our bodies as objects of desire or value to others, we need to value our own desires and our own subjective somatic experience.

So many women characters in novels are air-brushed-model-beautiful—big boobs, long legs, and so forth. There is nothing whatsoever wrong with big boobs and long legs, but we see so much of them in the media already. We need to see women of all shapes and sizes and ages and colors on the screen and on the page. We need to stop selling our apples. We need to taste them for ourselves, savor our own flavors.

Let your characters look like real people. Let them have bad tastes in their mouths and big moles on their arms and cellulite and dark circles under their eyes and real, beating hearts. Let them be beautiful, if the story calls for it, but let their beauty be unique, not carbon copy beauty. Writing is more vivid when it includes the rough patches of skin, not just satin fantasy flesh.

Apples and Oranges

It is easy for us to fall into the habit of comparing ourselves to others, whether we are judging thigh size or writing talent. It is easy to fall into a cycle of despair if we feel we don't measure up.

Our culture unfortunately teaches us that we are in competition with one another, that we are deeply lacking somehow if our breasts are smaller than the next woman's, or if our writing career lags behind the next writer's.

Pam Houston writes about a moment of awareness she had while walking down the street in Manhattan. "I realize with some horror," she recounts, "that for the last fifteen blocks I have been counting how many women have better and how many women have worse figures than I do. Did I say fifteen blocks? I meant fifteen years."

As long as we keep comparing ourselves, we can never feel fully at home in our own fruitflesh (and we can never fully connect with one another). It is just as silly as comparing apples and oranges. There is room in the world for all of our unique flavors and shapes. We can let ourselves be inspired, expanded by the amazing diversity of shape and voice, rather than diminished by it. We are all equally deserving of abundance.

The next time you find yourself thinking, "Her stomach is tighter than mine," or "She writes better metaphors than I'll ever be able to," take a pause. Close your eyes, and drop down into your body. Be aware of the rise and fall of your breath, the pulse of your heart. Remember that you—your fruitflesh, your writing voice—are unique and precious in this world. You are whole and perfect and beyond compare, right here, right now.

Sisterhood

Nobody in this lane, and nothing, nothing but blackberries,
Blackberries on either side, though on the right mainly,
A blackberry alley, going down in hooks, and a sea
Somewhere at the end of it, heaving. Blackberries
. . . fat

With blue-red juices. These they squander on my fingers.
I had not asked for such a blood sisterhood; they must love me.
Sylvia Plath, from "Blackberrying"

As women, we share a deep blood sisterhood through our bodies.

Write about a specific time when you have felt a visceral connection with other women. Perhaps it was while you were giving birth. Maybe it was during an Afro-Caribbean dance class or in the locker room at the community pool or in the middle of a gab session over lemon cake. Maybe it was the first time you touched your girlfriend's hair. How do you feel this sisterhood inside your body?

Women's relationships with each other can be deliciously layered. There can be tremendous power when women come together, a profound sense of community and support. Where do you go when you want to feel this connection? Have you ever been frustrated in your search?

Write an open letter to the sisterhood of women or, if you prefer, to a specific group of women or one woman in particular. Share your experiences of living in a woman's body; share how this experience connects you with other women who bleed and birth and walk through life in female flesh.

Naked Mangoes

Eat mangoes naked, lick the juice off your arms.
SARK, from *Succulent Wild Woman*

Do you enjoy being naked? Do you feel free without your clothes on, or do you feel vulnerable and self-conscious, even when you're alone? One of the greatest gifts we can give ourselves is the permission to feel at home inside our own skin. To be naked without worrying about our cellulite showing or our stomach pooching out when we sit down. To love each sweet inch of our bare fruit-flesh.

Sometimes it takes awhile to feel comfortable in the nude. Try to be bare a little bit every day, not just when you are taking a shower or bath. Read the paper naked, do the dishes. See how it feels to move around without any clothes on. Dance, skip, sashay around the house. Take SARK's advice—eat a juicy mango, or some other succulent fruit, and let it drip all over your skin. Revel in your nakedness!

Writing can be a kind of nakedness as well. We lay ourselves bare on the page, exposing our heart as well as our skin. This can be scary—reminiscent of those dreams where you show up for a test in high school and suddenly realize you're not wearing anything—but it can also be exhilarating. It is a brave act to strip all the way down, to not have anything left to hide.

Try writing in the nude, letting your naked body unite with your naked words. When you are unclothed, can your writing be equally bare, equally lush and present?

Breasts

Holding in my hand
a fig
It became my breast
soft, fleshy
converging to
the nipple

warehouse of sensation
enveloped in skin
marked like stretch marks
mapping its journey
from seed
to fruit
to sustenance
its darkness broke open
to color
a forest of poppies
yellowish
red
alive!
CATHERINE HONORA KINEAVY, from "The Fig"

When did your breasts first start to bud? How did you feel about them blossoming on your body, ripening into fruit?

Write about your breasts. Try not to place any judgments on them; just observe them tenderly and chronicle their sensations, their history. Look around at the amazing array of breasts in the world. Judith Werner reminds us how inside a sauna

. . . we are free to peer
with wonder at imperfect breasts: too small,
too large, pendulous, some with aureoles
like acorn cups around enormous fruit
or like collars on berries with nippled stems
. . . . .
. . . soon I
will blow dry, and walk back to the world
under wraps of its disdain, but here I am free,
having rarely loved my form since I was born.
from "In the Women's Spa"

When we see the true diversity of breast shape and size, we realize there is no such thing as an "imperfect" breast, no such thing as "too small" or "too large." As Clarissa Pinkola Estés writes, "Does it feed? Does it feel? It is a good breast." All our breasts are good, even if they don't look like the breasts we see in *Cosmo* or *Glamour.* We can write our way back into loving our form when we give our breasts the respect they deserve, both on and off the page. This is true for sick breasts as well as healthy ones; breast cancer, after all, affects one out of eight women. We can honor lost breasts by bringing them back to life on paper—celebrating their history, grieving their loss.

We can also celebrate the lactating breast in our work. If you breast-fed your children, did you find that the flow of milk from your body affected your creative flow as a writer? Write about the experience of being a fountain, a food factory, a pure creative source. Let your breasts tell their amazing dairy tales.

Rose Hips

Rose hips are the fruit that grows on rose stems after the blossoms fade. They are truly childbearing hips—seeds for new roses nestle inside their glossy skin.

Rose hips don't worry about how big they are. Why should we care about the size of our own hips?

Write about your hips. Exult in their fleshiness, their rhythm, the movements they allow. In her poem "Ode to My Hips," Leslea Newman writes, "I place my hands on these two hips / and let them speak the truth."

Tell the truth of your own hips. Write your own ode.

Cellulite

"What are these for?" Reina asks, poking through a bowl
of boiled avocado pits.
    Constancia cracks the pits open with the blade of a
knife and scrapes out the vegetal flesh. "Softens the
subcutaneous cells of the thigh. Reduces the appearance of
cellulite. Peel those peaches for me, will you?" ...
    Reina turns around, pulls up her terry-cloth cover-up
to reveal her puckered thighs. "Oye, chica, *since when*
did cellulite deter passion?"
CRISTINA GARCIA, from *The Agüero Sisters*

Cellulite is natural. Even the Venus of Willendorf has won-derfully rippled, abundant thighs. So why are these dimples and bulges so problematic for us? Why do we feel embarrassed, less sexy, if our thighs are not airbrush smooth?

Natalie Angier tells us that, evolutionarily speaking, the thighs and hips and buttocks are the best places to store excess flesh. It is truly "womanly fat," she says, its calories ready to be tapped during pregnancy and breast-feeding. There is nothing inherently wrong with cellulite, though the media tells us it looks bad.

With enough awareness, we can blast this programming out of our brains. We can learn to embrace our goddess form, each shim-mying inch of it. We can be fully sexual, passionate beings, even if we don't look like the current flavor of the day. We can, as Angier writes, "luxuriate in our bodies, our glorious, imperfect, sturdy, ludi-crous, womanly selves. Bare the pear. Giggle at the jiggle."

Write a letter to your cellulite (or any other perceived "imperfection" you may feel self-conscious about). Share your experiences trying to hide it, trying to get rid of it; let yourself delve deep into your problematic relationship with this part of your body. Writing about our cellulite (or our stretch marks, our scars, our wrinkles) can truly help us embrace those parts of ourselves, luxuriate in our whole bodies, giggle with pleasure at our jiggly dance.

Now give your cellulite a voice; have it write back to you. Let it tell you why it needs to live beneath your skin, why you need to accept—maybe even dare to love—its wild terrain.

Powerful, Wise, Vagina-Talking Women

As a piece of pomegranate are thy temples within thy locks.
SONG OF SOLOMON 6:7

Women's genitalia have often been depicted as fruit in myth and art throughout history. Pomegranates, figs, the clefts of peaches, the shape of the seeds when an apple has been halved—all have been compared to the fruits between our legs.

Until the past few decades, it was almost unheard of for women to write about their own fruitful sexual organs. Vaginas, clits, labia, and vulvas are now thankfully finding their rightful place in literature. If we're going to tell the truth about our bodies, we need to acknowledge and honor what's going on "down there."

In her incredible book, *The Vagina Monologues*, adapted from her stage show of the same name, Eve Ensler writes that she started the project because she was worried about vaginas, worried about the shame and silence that surround even the word itself. The book and show were culled from interviews in which she talked with over two hundred women, of all ages and backgrounds, about their vaginas. The result is amazing—honest, funny, touching, and, ultimately, empowering. Ensler writes,

> *And as more women say the word, saying it becomes less of*
> *a big deal; it becomes part of our language, part of our*
> *lives. Our vaginas become integrated and respected and*

sacred. They become part of bodies, connected to our minds,
fueling our spirits. And the shame leaves and the violation
stops, because vaginas are visible and real, and they are
connected to powerful, wise, vagina-talking women.

It's your turn to be a "powerful, wise, vagina-talking (or writing) woman"! Write about your vagina, your vulva. Look at yourself with a hand mirror as you write. Don't let yourself write any negative words that you may have attached to your genitals before—*disgusting, smelly,* and so forth. Find a way to celebrate your fruited loins on the page.

Writing and Other Secretions

Like a fruit, our bodies leak all kinds of juices.

A. E. Housman once said, "If I were obliged . . . to name the class of things to which (poetry) belongs, I should call it a secretion."

Writing that comes from the body is truly like a secretion, oozing organically from our deepest places. It can pack the same power as a secretion, too—dazzling as a squirt of adrenaline.

Secretions and body fluids are not always looked upon kindly in the real world. Especially when a person is HIV-positive.

Irene Borger, founder of the AIDS Project Los Angeles Writer's Workshop, has created an exercise called "reclaiming body fluids." She has workshop participants choose three body fluids and then list a memory-associated person, place, activity, and age for each fluid. Each person chooses one memory from this list and writes for thirty minutes. By doing this, people are able to recapture a sense of the body's dignity. The feelings of shame and anger that are often attached to HIV-positive body fluids can be replaced, through writing, by feelings of respect for the memory and meaning encoded in all of our cells, all of our secretions.

Using Borger's template, write about one of your own body fluids. Consider saliva, sweat, snot, the *spinnbarkeit* that gushes when you ovulate, blood, urine, the juices of desire. Let the words ooze out as naturally as any hormone, any endorphin, anything our bodies need in moments of pain or fear or love.

Period

Yes, I want to talk at length about Men-
struation. Or my period.
Or the rag as you so lovingly put it.
All right then.

I'd like to mention my rag time.

Gelatinous. Steamy
and lovely to the light to look at
like a good glass of burgundy. Suddenly
I'm artist each month.
The star inside this like a ruby.
Fascinating bits of sticky
I-don't-know-what-stuff.
The afterbirth without the birth.
The gobs of strawberry jam.
Membrane stretchy like
saliva in your hand.
. . . .
I'd like to dab my fingers
in my inkwell
and write a poem across the wall.
"A Poem of Womanhood"
Now wouldn't that be something?
SANDRA CISNEROS, from "Down There"

It has only been in the past few decades that women have felt the freedom to write about their body's cycles. In 1966, Anne Sexton broke things open with her poem "Menstruation at Forty." We still have a lot of catching up to do. Every aspect of our physical experience is worth acknowledging. We shouldn't deny our own blood.

Write about your period. Your first period. Your most recent period. Any in between that stand out in your memory. If you have reached menopause, write about that experience. Weave your own menstruation creation story; wrap your reproductive cycle in myth.

You may want to write with a red pen or a berry or a pomegranate seed or even, like Sandra Cisneros suggests, your own blood. Write your own "Poem of Womanhood." Find a way to explore and celebrate your body's monthly cycles on the page.

Have you noticed whether your creative flow is in rhythm with your menstrual cycle? Some women find that they are most creative in the middle of their cycle (when we are most fertile!) and most contemplative during their periods. Other women find their periods unleash a flow of words. Listen to your body; how do your own natural rhythms influence your work?

Peeling Oranges

LIDDY'S ORANGE

The rind lies on the table where Liddy has left it
torn into pieces the size of petals and
curved like petals, rayed out like a
full-blown rose, one touch will make it come apart.
The lining of the rind is wet and chalky as
Devonshire cream, rich as the glaucous
lining of a boiled egg, all that protein
cupped in the ripped shell. And the navel,

torn out carefully,
lies there like a fat gold
bouquet, and the scar of the stem, picked out
with her nails, and still attached to the white
thorn of the central integument,
lies down on the careful heap, a tool laid
down at the end of a ceremony.
All here speaks of ceremony,
the sheen of acrid juice, which is all that is
left of the flesh, the pieces lying in
profound order like natural order,
as if this simply happened, the way her
life at 13 looks like something that's just
happening, unless you see her
standing over it, delicately clawing it open.
SHARON OLDS

Remember back to when you stood at the gateway of adolescence—the gateway that led to your womanhood, to yourself as a sexual being. Was this threshold one you were eager to pass through, or was it dark and foreboding, a scary prospect?

Write about yourself when you had one leg firmly planted in girlhood, the other venturing into new womanly frontiers. Did you have guides along the way—your mother, your friends—or did you navigate the unknown territory solo? What were some of your expectations? What did you imagine you'd be like as a teenager, as a grown woman? Have you stepped into the picture you had formed of yourself?

Is there anything you would want to tell yourself as a girl approaching young womanhood? Write your younger self a letter; let her know who you have become; give her a lamp to help her find her way.

Further Peelings

Your fingers pry the skin of a navel orange
Releasing tiny explosions of spicy oil.
You place peeled disks of gold in a bizarre pattern
On my white body. Rearranging, you bend and bite
The disks to release further their eager scent.
I say, "Stop, you're tickling," my eye still on the page.
Aromas of groves arise. Through green leaves
Glow the lofty snows. Through red lips
Your white teeth close on a translucent segment.
Your face over my face eclipses The World's Illusion.
Pulp and juice pass into my mouth from your mouth.
We laugh against each other's lips.

VIRGINIA HAMILTON ADAIR, from "Peeling an Orange"

Virginia Hamilton Adair's poem displays a woman deeply rooted in her sexual, sensual self, deeply at home with intimacy. How do we get from the uncertainty of adolescence to this place of knowing and ease?

Write about your own ripening, from the first glimmers of your sexuality to your present sensual life. How did you get from there to here? Write about the landmarks along the way. When was the first time you felt like a sexual being? You may want to write about your first awkward sexual experiences, maybe your first satisfying sexual experiences. If you are still in the process of making peace with your sexuality, you may want to write about your frustrations, your fears; you may try to map out ways in which you can move toward fulfillment.

Write with as much or as little detail as you feel comfortable with. You can write a blow-by-blow report or a more atmospheric, metaphoric account from deep within the experience.

Desire

HONEYSUCKLE

Helpless as an apricot in heavy sun
blushing into softness
or a sliced strawberry
drawing sugar into its flesh,

she turns on the couch to face east,
his house, she eats the limp scraps
of honeysuckle dropped on the chocolate box,
drifts over midnight wet grass

as if drowned by a single star—
feels a cool leaf edge, unmelting, draw her arm.
Puts all five fingers into a rose
and makes it open too.

SARAH LINDSAY

What do you desire? How does your body open to its own hunger?

There are times when the state of desire permeates the surrounding world, coloring everything we see, touch, hear, smell, giving everything the sudden power to stir us.

Imagine someone just gave you a pair of fruitflesh glasses that tinge your vision with desire. Slip them on and look around you. How do these lenses change the way you see the grain of the hardwood floor, the curl of the wisteria vine outside your window, the blowsy pile of paper on your desk? Write about what you see. Now take the glasses off, and record your perception. How do the two accounts differ?

Desire is not always sexual, although it is informed by sexual energy. Writing that stems from this erotic sensibility is not always, by definition, erotica. It is writing suffused with an openness to sensation, to the body and the body's connection with the world that surrounds it.

What stirs you? What raises your brow, makes you lick your lips, causes your heart to skip a beat? Write a list of things—the curl of a flower, the scent of mango or the sea—that cause desire to well up within you. What are the erotics of your world?

Thinking About Love

I have loved other men since, taken
them into my mouth like a warm vowel,
lain beneath them and watched their irises
float like small worlds in their open eyes.

But this man pressed his thumb
toward the tail of my spine
like he was entering
China, or a ripe papaya
so that now when I think of love,
I think of this.
DORIANNE LAUX, from "China"

What do you think of when you think of love? Is there a defining moment in your life that speaks "love" to you in a clear, true way? This can be sexual love, familial love, love for a pet, a place, a poem—whatever kind of love makes your heart hum strong.

How does love inhabit your body? Do different types of love sing through your fruitflesh in different octaves? *Love* is such a huge word in itself. When we write about love, it is good to find details that can boil the word, the feeling, down to specific moments—the movement of a lover's thumb, the way your heart swells when you watch your child sleep, the tingle in your shoulder blades as you crack open a favorite book. . . . Write about your own ripe experiences, your own touchstones—lodestones—of love.

A Melon for Oshun

In Santería, there is a beautiful, fruitful ritual women practice to ensure motherhood. Women who wish to become pregnant consult Oshun, the orisha, or goddess, of the rivers. Oshun is considered the Venus of the Santería pantheon. The abdominal area is her sacred territory.

In this particular ritual, a woman buys a honeydew melon in Oshun's name. She writes a letter to Oshun on a brown piece of paper, expressing her desire for a child. She then slides the note into the melon through a small slit cut into the rind. She wraps the melon in a yellow cloth and burns a white candle. Five days later, the woman brings the melon to the river, Oshun's home, along with twenty-seven cents, and offers it to the orisha.

The urge to write can be very similar to the urge to conceive a child. You can practice your own version of this melon ritual, so long as you enter the experience with respect for its powerful origin.

Rather than writing a wish for a child when you practice this ritual, write down what you wish to give birth to as a writer, what your deepest desires are for your creative work, then slip your words into the melon. Try to really feel the presence of Oshun before you give the fruit up to the river.

Pro-Creation

Our bellies are eight-month fruits
fabulous with weightlessness.
We have entered summer like a state of pasture,
pregnancy like a state of mind so full
nothing else can be.
Sharing this is simple: the surprise of a tomato
still perfect after days in a pocket.
Here is the circle made flesh.

BARBARA RAS, from "Pregnant Poets Swim Lake Tarleton,
New Hampshire"

A pregnant woman fully understands how the belly is our
deepest source of creativity. Our procreative center is our creative
center as well. We can be pregnant with a baby or pregnant with an
idea, a vision, a song. Our hearts and bodies dilate to let life pass
through us in many forms.

If you have been pregnant, write about the experience of car-
rying life—each trimester, each change of belly and breast, skin and
hair and mood and walk. Did your belly button open like a flower?
Did your nipples darken? Did you develop a linea negra—a dark
animal seam down the center of your belly? How did you feel when
the baby somersaulted and hiccuped inside? Write about the birth
itself. What did your body teach you through labor, through push-
ing, through the moment when the baby's shoulders slithered out
between your legs? How has the creativity of your body informed
your creativity on the page?

Think about a time when you have felt pregnant in a sym-
bolic way—a story or poem or play kicking under your skin, push-
ing its way into the light. Did you know when the piece was first
conceived? Did you give yourself proper prenatal care, nurturing
yourself while the work continued to grow inside you?

Our Lady with the Pomegranate

According to *The Woman's Encyclopedia of Myths and Secrets*, Hera, the Greek mother goddess, is worshiped at a certain shrine in Capaccio Vecchio as "Our Lady with the Pomegranate." She sits, in statue form, with a child on one arm and a pomegranate in her opposite hand, "inviting contemplation of the miracle of her bringing forth life." The shrine was rebuilt in the twelfth century C.E. People still make pilgrimage there and, as in ancient times, lay little boats filled with flowers at her feet.

Mothers who write are very much like "Our Lady with the Pomegranate," balancing our children on one arm, our creative fruits on the other. Sometimes the two work together beautifully. Other times balance seems impossible. As hard as it can get, we need to remember how lucky we are to hold such riches in our arms. These gifts can be a challenge, but at least the challenge is one that lies close to our hearts, our bellies, close to the core of our lives. Either way we turn, we are witness to the miracle—we embody the miracle—of bringing forth life.

All women writers, whether mothers or not, engage in a balancing act. We have to juggle day jobs with our creative work, family responsibilities with time for ourselves, mashing potatoes with making poems. The trick lies in finding a way to allow these different aspects of ourselves to nourish, rather than to oppose, one another—a task that is not always easy. When we even try to keep all our plates spinning at once, we become miracle workers. People should throw flowers at our feet.

Bottled Up, Ready to Bloom

In her bottled up is a woman peppery as curry,
a yam of a woman of butter and brass,
compounded of acid and sweet like a pineapple,
like a hand grenade set to explode,
like goldenrod ready to bloom.
MARGE PIERCY, from "The woman in the ordinary"

What woman is bottled up inside of you? What woman is ready to explode or bloom under your skin? Is this woman angry? Passionate? Fearless? At peace?

At my thirtieth birthday party, I passed out name tags and asked everyone to write down the name of who or what they wanted to be. One friend wrote she wanted to be the layer of sugar on top of broiled grapefruit. Another friend wanted to be Diana Ross. Another simply wrote "Sane." My first impulse was to write something poetic—"the light that glimmers on a hummingbird's wing" or some similarly lovely and selfless thing—but then another voice asserted itself inside me. I ended up writing "Loud Bossy Chick" on my name tag. A few of my friends thought I was making reference to them—I know some wonderfully loud bossy chicks—but I meant the firebrand that lives somewhere inside my shy, quiet skin.

Write from the voice of the woman who simmers inside you, the woman who hasn't been fully born, fully released, yet. What does this woman want to tell you? How can you help her find her way into the world?

Fruitflesh Meditation: Apple

Apples are probably the most widely mythologized fruit. They are rife, and ripe, with associations, some of them quite contradictory. Eve's apple represents temptation, while an apple for the teacher is a wholesome token of appreciation. Apples represent knowledge; they represent death. They represent sexuality in Tantric ritual; they represent the Virgin Mary in Christian iconography.

Slice an apple in half, across its belly. Note the star shape of the seeds inside. Take a bite of the fruit. Taste how all of the apple's contradictions come together to form a perfect whole.

What are some of the contradictions you hold inside your skin? Don't deny them on the page; they make life interesting, more richly textured. You are full of star seeds and dazzling shifting sands; you pack a wholesome crunch as well as slippery skins of desire. Your fruitflesh unites all of it in perfect, delicious balance.

PART NINE

Seeds

. . . I like the idea of a fruit already delicious
giving birth to sweeter riches from its oval kernel . . .

LIN MAX,
from "Stone Fruit"

Writing can give birth to itself, over and over again. Let your work yield seeds for even further expression, even greater self-knowledge, even deeper self-love.

Fruitflesh Meditation: Watermelon

A watermelon is a generous fruit. It grows large and lush on the vine. Its rind is smooth green tiger skin, its flesh a pulpy pink heart.

Slice into a watermelon. Look at the fruit glistening inside. Its flesh almost falls right into your lap, it is so willing to share itself. Grab handfuls of the fruit—let the juice leak through your fingers and onto your chin when you take one big, glorious bite after another. Press the sweet flesh against the roof of your mouth, releasing its mellifluous flavor. Lick the sticky pulp from your palms, your forearms. Slurp the fruit all the way down to the rind. Arrange the seeds before you; take a good look. Isn't it amazing that such plush abundance can grow from these glossy little buttons, these teardrop onyx beads?

When you write, be generous. Share yourself freely. Your words are that much more delicious when they unfold from an open heart.

Body Paint

In *The Pillow Book of Sei Shonagon*, written around 965 C.E., the author includes, in her list of "Adorable Things," "the face of a child drawn on a melon." In the movie *The Pillow Book*, a woman has a fetish for being written on, just like a melon, with a calligraphy brush.

Write a poem on a melon.

Write upon your own fruitflesh.

Using washable marker or body paint or lipstick or chalk or fruit, write a love poem to your thigh on your thigh. Write "I am a writer!" on your belly. Or just write single words on various body parts—*Beautiful* on the hip you are trying to appreciate, *Leopard* on your breast. Make sense, or don't. Have fun. Use your body as a blank page. Use your lover's body as a blank page. Write love poems on each other to each other. You can choose to write about your own body writing explorations later, or you can keep the experience self-contained, letting your skin remember the language it held.

Weight

A fruit is not afraid of its own weight. It grows into its own skin fully. It is whole, each part of its body equally alive.

In writing, we need to not be afraid of our own weight. This is different from scale weight, although we shouldn't be afraid of that, either. In writing, weight has more to do with intention, attention, focus. When you read something, you can feel whether a writer has put her full weight, her full commitment, into the writing. There is an integrity about this kind of writing, a breathtaking honesty. It registers in your body, can alter your heartbeat, send cold bolts of adrenaline up your spine as you read it. You can also feel when the writer has held back some of her weight, allowing her writing to skim along the surface, afraid to call forth its own power. Your own body won't be nearly as engaged; it's like reaching out to shake someone's hand and getting a dead fish on your palm. A writer who uses her full weight gives you a hearty handshake in return and may even crush some of your fingers in the process.

Choose a subject that you know a little something about and have a modicum of interest in, whether it's gardening or welding or Skee-Ball. Write a few sentences about this subject without letting yourself get fully engaged in the material; give as dry and detached an account as possible (which may, in fact, lead to some lovely writing). Now bring your full body to the subject, and write a few more sentences. This doesn't mean you need to add a lot of exclamation points or superlatives. Just allow your writing to be muscular, to come from deep inside the fiber of the experience. Can you see the difference between the two accounts?

Wordwalk

Today I walked and felt the words
pressing into my feet
with fir cones and pebbles.

I've been told the best poets
write of Aeschylus and Homer
whose faces to me are chiseled bronze—
hard gods.

I'd rather stumble against tree roots,
splay out my fingers
in pine sap.

What I don't know
I am learning
from the sweetness of huckleberries.
KATHERINE G. BOND, "Wordwalk"

As writers, we need to read as much as we can, to soak in the words of others until we are ready to burst with our own torrent of language. Books are infinitely precious. It is important to run our fingers along the spines of books, to spread their pages open in our laps, to inhale the scent of the paper, the ink. We need to luxuriate in libraries, journey through journals, let words sing us to sleep.

It is equally important, however, for us to put the books and magazines down and engage our senses fully with the world. Our work will be all the richer if we soak in scent and sight and sound as eagerly as we soak in the printed page.

Try to spend some time outside—preferably in a natural setting, somewhere removed from any human chatter, any hints of human language. Stumble on tree roots. Splay your fingers out in pine sap. Feel the way your skin responds to the temperature, the brush of leaves. Let yourself become all eyes, all nose, all tongue, all nerve ending. Let your body drink in the environment; become a wordless part of it. Let the sweetness of huckleberries teach you all you need to know. If words should happen to press into your feet along with the pebbles, welcome them, but don't feel the need to write as you walk. Later, you can record the different ways the wilderness wrote itself into your flesh.

Cravings

. . . our need for oranges goes beyond craving.
COLETTE, from "Flora and Pomona"

Do you crave anything right now? A ripe peach, bursting with juice? The crunch of an apple? A salted plum?

I once read something about the distinction between craving food that "hums" to you and food that "beckons." When a food *hums*, it means the craving is coming from within your body; it is a food that will truly satisfy you. A food that *beckons*, on the other hand, comes from the outside, like when you see a cake in a bakery window and decide you need it right then and there. These beckoning foods will taste good but will not satisfy any inner hunger. When we are in touch with the foods that hum to us, we will eat what our bodies need, and we will stop when our bodies are satisfied. If we eat only the foods that beckon to us, though, we will never truly be sated. We will stuff ourselves to the gills because we are not in touch with what our bodies truly want and need.

This is true with writing, as well. When I write a story that hums so loudly inside me it has turned my whole body into a tuning fork, I am deeply satisfied. If I try to write something I think I "should" write, though, if the impulse comes from somewhere outside myself, the writing can feel empty, unsatisfying.

At the Los Angeles Times Book Festival in 1998, I asked Isabel Allende how living in a woman's body affects her voice as a writer. At first she said she can only write in a woman's body because she doesn't know how to write in a man's body. ("I wouldn't know what to do with that thing!" she said.) Then she went on to say that people all over the world ask her to write their stories, but when she tries to, she can't. She can only write the stories that resonate organically in her own body. The ones that hum.

What stories or poems are humming inside you right now? Shove the beckoning ones aside, and indulge yourself. Write what you truly want to write, what you truly *need* to write. Anything else is fluff, a cake in a bakery window—beautiful, maybe, but full of empty calories. Write the words that will nourish and sustain you.

Patience

Learning Courage

How many pears will that tree attempt, how many
give up to gravity's insistence? All winter
you parted the curtains
as if opening your hands in prayer, raised the shade
like incense sent skyward.
You watched for first signs: a thickening
of branch, a swelling into bud,
a signal that the days
do more than accumulate. The first
explosions began on the southwestern branches, leaves
edged out blossoms and a new swelling began,
clustered, purposeful. This tree has no need
for you, your doubts—its attention focused on each
beginning, sending water along each arcing branch
each leaf a factory, everything
working together toward fruition.

Elizabeth Austen

Waiting is an integral part of the writing process. The silences are just as important as prolific spurts of inspiration. Sometimes our stories need to gestate inside our bodies, growing slowly, gathering sweetness, before they're ready to bloom. It takes courage to trust these fallow periods. Even when you are in the throes of self-doubt, remember that your senses are patiently and continually taking in fresh material. Your breath is constantly guiding you with its rhythm. Your words will find a way to come to the surface when they are ripe. Everything is working together toward fruition.

Comfort

Comfort me with apples.
Song of Solomon 2:5

What comforts you? A warm bath? A cup of tea and a cookie? Your lover's arms? A friend's voice on the phone?

Bring that comfort to the page. Write about the things that make you feel safe and warm and fuzzy, the things that bring peace to your body and mind. Whether you love to wrap yourself in flannel or silk, eat a bowl of ice cream, pet your cat, sing along to your favorite music, or dig your hands into the soil of your garden, let your sense of contentment and pleasure seep onto the paper. When you are feeling frazzled, you can look at what you've written and let the words soothe you like a lullaby.

Joy

O poor [woman] who has pledged
To thus spend [her] time
Without fruit, joy, and pleasure!

ANNA OWENA HOYERS, sixteenth century, from "Brief Reflections on
the Marriage of Old Women, Since God Has Nothing to Do with It"

We are poor, indeed, when we don't allow our bodies to
experience all the pleasures that are our birthright. Write about a
time when your body accepted its own inherent richness, when you
felt completely at home and joyful in your skin. If you can't think of
a specific time, make one up, or write about a fictional character
who revels in simple movement, in simple, playful embodiment.

Better yet, find a way to experience this kind of joy! Climb a
tree, cartwheel in your backyard, knead some bread dough and
watch the tendons and muscles in your arms and hands awaken.
Roll around in the morning dew, dance until sweat flies off your
hair, be like a cat and curl up on a comfy chair in a puddle of sun-
light. When you are ready, write about your body's joy. Let these
pleasures act as seeds for further acceptance and delight.

Humble Apologies

THIS IS JUST TO SAY
I have eaten
the plums
that were in
the icebox

and which
you were probably saving
for breakfast

Forgive me
they were delicious
so sweet
and so cold
William Carlos Williams

William Carlos Williams wrote a great apology poem. Now it's your turn.

Write an apology poem (or letter) to your body. Unlike William Carlos Williams, though, don't apologize for eating. Women apologize way too often for eating. Apologize for all the things you *haven't* eaten, all the pleasures you have resisted, all the things you've denied your body. Be honest but compassionate with yourself. Promise your body a special treat to make up for all the times you have forsaken your fruitflesh.

If you feel like it, for fun, also write a response poem to William Carlos Williams. Let him know just how you feel about his taking those plums that were rightfully yours!

Features

I once heard two shepherds arguing over which was
Rachel's best feature, a game I, too, had played. For me,
the most wonderful detail of Rachel's perfection was her
cheeks, which were high and tight on her face, like figs.
When I was a baby, I used to reach for them, trying to
pluck the fruit that appeared when she smiled. When I
realized there was no having them, I licked her instead,
hoping for a taste.
Anita Diamant, from *The Red Tent*

What is your own favorite feature? What part of your body do you absolutely love? Your belly button? Your ankles? The little crease beneath your bottom lip? The graceful stretch of muscle that swoops between your neck and shoulder? Write an ode that celebrates the part of your body you appreciate most. Be elaborate with your praise!

What features do you particularly love on people you know—your sister's eyebrows? The small of your lover's back? Your mother's hands? Write an ode to each of these cherished parts. You may want to share what you've written with the objects of your affection; it may help them appreciate their own bodies more fully!

Love Poem

CELEBRATION OF THE BODY

I love this body of mine that has lived a life,
its amphora contour soft as water,
my hair gushing out of my skull,
my face a glass goblet on its delicate stem
rising with grace from shoulders and collarbone.

I love my back studded with ancient stars,
the bright mounds of my breasts,
fountains of milk, our species' first food,
my protruding ribcage, my yielding waist,
my belly's fullness and warmth.

I love the lunar curve of my hips
shaped by various gestations,
the great curling wave of my buttocks,
my legs and feet, on which the temple stands.

I love my bunch of dark petals and secret fur
keeper of heaven's mysterious gate,
to the damp hollow from which blood flows
and the water of life.

This body of mine that can hurt and get ill,
that oozes, coughs, sweats,
secretes humours, faeces, saliva,
grows tired, old and worn out.

Living body, one solid link to secure
the unending chain of bodies.
I love this body made of pure earth,
seed, root, sap, flower and fruit.

DAISY ZAMORA, translated by Dinah Livingston

Now that you have sung the praises of your favorite feature, write a love poem or letter to your entire body. It may be hard for some of us to express love for our bodies when we have been taught to hate our own flesh. This exercise, this book, can help you begin to heal that relationship. Every inch of our bodies deserves our love.

Think about the parts of the body you apologized to earlier, the parts you've treated poorly, unfairly. Write a love poem or letter to those parts. If you don't like how your thighs look, think about their strength, their power, the way they can wrap themselves around a lover. If you're not happy with the shape of your nose, think about all the amazing aromas it allows you to enjoy. Let these grateful acknowledgments become seeds for you to express love for your whole body, in all its imperfect glory.

Why Don't You Marry It?

In an episode of *Pee Wee's Playhouse*, Pee Wee can't stop talking about how much he loves fruit salad. Someone teases him, "If you love it so much, why don't you marry it?" True to the inspired lunacy of the show, Pee Wee ends up marrying a bowl of fruit salad in an elaborate ceremony. The bowl, of course, is decked out in a lovely veil.

What fruit do you love so much that you would want to marry it? Choose a fruit that in some way expresses who you want to be as a writer, perhaps the fruit you wrote about earlier in your (wo)manifesto. Have a private little ceremony, and pronounce yourself woman and mango, woman and plum. Let the ritual be as serious or as silly as you want it to be. As you marry the fruit, you marry your own creative potential. Kiss your beloved, then devour it in glorious consummation. No need for wedding rings; the symbol of your union will be the juicy movement of your fingers as you write, fueled by the fruit's creative juice. You may, however, want to keep one of the seeds on your desk, or glue some of them into a collage, to remind yourself that the fruit will always be a part of you.

The Edge

I enter where I've entered before—
a dozen times, maybe more—a rhythm

catches me quickly: a fine push and glide,
muscles contracting, relaxing in time

with my breathing; then, pumping my arms,
holding my spread thighs apart—straining

with effort—I herringbone-climb to the ridge,
where, finally, I can begin. Sweating,

heart pounding, cheeks flushed and tingling,
I watch the blood-orange sun stain the snow.
JOANNE HAYHURST, from "What Daphne Said"

When have you pushed your body to the edge? When has your body dissolved into sweat and pulse and flush? After a race? A night of dancing? A particularly amorous encounter with a lover?

Write about what it feels like to reach the far limits of your endurance, your own apex of physical exertion. Write about how you got there.

In her poem about skiing, Joanne Hayhurst chose to write the piece in couplets—two-line stanzas—which look like a series of two skis stacked together. Think about ways in which you can frame your experience so the form matches the content. Can your words visually run, dance, make love on the page, while they speak of your physical efforts?

Repeating Themes

For other fruits my father was indifferent.
He'd point at the cherry trees and say,
"See those? I wish they were figs."
In the evenings he sat by my bed
weaving folktales like vivid little scarves.
They always involved a fig tree.
Even when it didn't fit, he'd stick it in.
Once Joha was walking down the road and he saw a fig tree.

Or, he tied his donkey to a fig tree and went to sleep.
Or, later when they caught and arrested him,
his pockets were full of figs.
NAOMI SHIHAB NYE, from "My Father and the Fig Tree"

A couple of years ago, I became aware that most of the stories I had written contained at least one pivotal scene in a hospital. I spent quite a bit of time in hospitals as a teenager; placing my characters there helped me digest my own experience. Through my fiction I was able to begin to translate that chaos and pain into something cathartic, something I could shape and own. In a similar way now, I keep writing about the body, through the body, writing myself deeper and deeper into my own flesh.

After you have been writing for a while, you will most likely find that certain themes crop up repeatedly in your work, like fig trees. You may keep returning to your first love or your mother's death or your childhood neighborhood in your poems, or all of your stories may revolve around themes of forgiveness or redemption or women coming into their own power. Unless you feel like you've written yourself into a rut, don't worry about repeating yourself in this way. Sometimes we need to reexplore the same territory, from different angles, until we've processed it fully, integrated it into our consciousness.

If you find yourself revisiting the same images, the same themes, look at them closely. What can they tell you about yourself? You may want to do a freewrite about why these things are so crucial to you and your work. Then try writing them from a fresh perspective. Instead of writing about a fig tree, you can write from the viewpoint of the bird who builds a nest in its branches or the bug who gnaws a hole in its trunk; you can write from the perspective of the fig tree itself. When you approach the subject from as many angles as possible, you have a better chance of shedding light upon the real heart of the matter.

Artifacts

The woman is in love with the poem. It is a short poem,
carved in the shape of a deer, from ice. Its antlers are
twigs, coated with silver. Each hoofprint reflects
movement, the light of changing stars. It is a poem of
snow, its story flung, like a fistful of winter, across house,
forest, field. But it is not a cold poem. Somewhere deep
within the deer's body a small red berry quivers, names
itself as heart.
ALISON TOWNSEND, from "Lifeline"

Are your poems made of ice? Cashmere? Raw meat? Does each essay you write feel as solid as a tooth? Are some of your stories strong and fluid rivers, while others seem to be made of parched straw? Imagine each piece of your writing has suddenly been transformed into an artifact—a fact of art, a tangible, three-dimensional object in the world. What would each one look like? Would each have a scent? A texture? A temperature? Would one be a spoon, one a clover blossom, one a jagged cliff?

Choose one piece of your writing, and detail the artifact it has been transformed into, using all your senses. ("My poem is a redbrick building with geraniums in two of its windows and a watchdog snarling at the door. . . ." or "My story is a feather bed; the scent of apricot nectar wafts from the sheets. . . .")

What sort of artifact do you hope to leave behind as a writer? Can you write a poem or story that has the heft, the contours, of the thing you have chosen?

Fruition Rituals

[When we moved into our house] I immediately went
and bought fruit trees for each of my children, and in
keeping with my Jamaican tradition, transferred the soil
from the houseplant in which their umbilical cords had
been planted to the soil that surrounded their fruit trees.
The trees represent the continuity of their lives, just as the
orange tree back in Jamaica represents mine.
OPAL PALMER ADISA, from "Working in My Garden:
The Aesthetic Nature of Therapy"

Just as we can mark the beginning of a writing project with a ritual, we can also use ritual to honor its fruition. The birth of a long-awaited book or poem or story or paragraph, even, is something well worth celebrating. Every time she publishes a poem, Opal Palmer Adisa buys herself a new plant. She is surrounded by the proof of her fecundity, her creative power breathing green all around her.

When we do something kind for ourselves after we open ourselves to creation, we create the momentum, the affirmation, for that creation to continue. Like planting an umbilicus beneath a fruit tree, we acknowledge how our creativity will feed further growth.

What do you want to do to honor the fruition of your own creative process? Do you want to eat something exquisite? Plant a tree? Go to the shore and find a perfect stone for your windowsill? Or do you want to just dive right into the next project, your creative juices the only ritual you'll ever need?

Submission

Fruit is the final stage of the unfolding of a plant.
With its fruit, the plant in a sense reaches its fullest
self-development, attains its ultimate goal. The
rest is up to the birds, the bees, the wind, and the rain.
ANNEMARIE COLBIN, *Food and Healing*

At some point, if you haven't yet already, you may decide you want to send your writing out into the world. Your story is as good as it's going to be; like a fruit, it has reached its "fullest self-development." It deserves to be read.

The path to publication is not always straightforward. Expect to hit a few potholes along the way. Rejections are an integral part of the process. Try not to take them personally. A rejection does not mean your work is worthless or that you are. *Two Girls Review* in Portland, Oregon, uses a wonderful form rejection letter that all writers should heed. It says:

No.

editorial choices are fucking
arbitrary. you know it, we know it.
that's why you should not take this
no as anything but some jerk-off's
idea about what fit and what didn't
fit this go round. our decisions are
no reflection on the merit of your
work—they are as full of shit as our
own colossal egos. these are
important: hands, ideas, mouths,
words, images.

our advice?
be relentless.

All rejection letters should be so honest.

There are steps you can take toward being relentless, if publication is something you truly desire. *Poets & Writers* magazine is a wonderful resource for writers. Every issue of the journal is packed with calls for submission from journals and anthologies looking for stories, poems, and essays, sometimes with specific themes. Send for sample issues of literary journals, to get a taste for what they print. Submit to magazines and publishers you share a real affinity with, ones that publish work that resonates with your own. Send your very best work only—work that feels ready to leave the nest. Send a neatly printed copy, and be sure to enclose a self-addressed, stamped envelope for the reply.

The best way to be relentless is to be relentless about the creative process, not the finished product. It's important to detach yourself from your work after you slide it into an envelope. Mail off that piece, then start writing another. Just as Annemarie Colbin writes above about fruit, remember that writing itself is its own fulfillment. It is the writing, not publication, that constitutes your final stage of fruitful unfolding. The publication process is out of your hands. *The rest is up to the birds, the bees, the wind, and the rain.* What is in your hands is the creative process. Keep the juices flowing. Trust that your work will find a home when the time and place is right.

Seedlings

Writing is self-propagating. A fruit holds the seeds of future growth inside its skin. So do we. The more we write, the more we create seeds for further writing.

When you're writing, sometimes an image or character or sentence will appear and demand its own poem or essay or story. Stay mindful when this happens. Set these seeds aside so they can sprout when they are ready. Occasionally these kernels are so persistent, it's wise to drop what you're working on and follow their lead. A fruit that is not completely sound will often yield some very fruitful seeds.

It's also good to mine seeds from the fruits we find delicious. The process of writing *Fruitflesh* has been an incredible one for me. Now it is spawning further journeys. While working on this book, I became acutely aware of some of my own deep contradictions. My voice on the page is loud and clear and confident, but I am not nearly as comfortable with my own voice in the world. I am now launching into an exploration of creative balance, on and off the page, a process that so far has been both fun and profound. *Fruitflesh* provided the seeds for this project, which in turn, I know, will generate even more seeds.

What seedlings are sprouting inside you? Let them grow; continue to nourish them as they push their way into the light. Keep listening to your own inner impulses. Let yourself be witness to your own gorgeous unfolding.

Fruitflesh Meditation: Custard Apple

The custard apple, or cherimoya, is absolutely luscious. The jade skin looks vaguely reptilian. The silky flesh inside is the color of cream. Seeds—large and smooth and chocolate brown—sit quietly throughout the fruit.

Cut the custard apple in half. Dig a spoon into the soft fruit, and slip it into your mouth. Swoon to its vanilla-mango-pineapple flavor. Let the seeds slide across your tongue, click against your teeth. Note how each one holds a whole tree, a whole potential crop of fruit, inside its calm exterior. Don't swallow these cherimoya seeds. Spit them out with great gusto. Let them find their way into the world. Plant one, if you desire. Remember that every time you write, you create seeds for further expression.

Let your writing ooze with sensuality, rich as custard fruit. Give your fruitflesh the chance to express itself, reclaim itself, honor and celebrate itself over and over again, both in your body and on the page. You are your own source of creative renewal. May your path home be a juicy one.

Acknowledgments

This book did not drop into my lap, fully formed like an apple. Many hands and hearts helped bring *Fruitflesh* into being, and it is a great pleasure to be able to acknowledge them now.

Special thanks to friends—Kate Anger, Amy Printup, Lee Peckler, Jianda Johnson, Kristin Kucia-Stauder, Peggy Hong—and family—Elizabeth, Arlene, Buzz, and Magdalene Brandeis—who read early drafts of this book and offered invaluable suggestions and encouragement. Thanks to everyone who helped me search for delicious writings about fruit, especially Robert Wynne, who surprised me with a veritable cornucopia of poems; John Fox, who introduced me to Charles Olson's wonderful "roots" poem; and Peggy for reminding me to look at, and absorb, Marilyn Krysl's wise words about the dark. All my friends and relations have been so generous with love and support; I am overflowing with appreciation for each and every one of you, and wish I could list all your names!

Catherine Kineavy, I can't thank you deeply enough. You have opened more doors for me than you will ever know. I am so grateful to continue to share this journey with you.

Abundant gratitude to my parents for nurturing my love of writing from the time I was four years old. Thanks and admiration to my sister, who as a midwife in training bears regular witness to the power of women's bodies and continually inspires me with her own power. Endless hugs and kisses to my husband, Matt McGunigle, for having faith in the value of my work even when it didn't put any fruit on the table. Extra squeezes to our kids, Arin and Hannah, for keeping me grounded and reminding me to be silly every once in awhile.

I am grateful to have been part of such vibrant learning communities at the University of Redlands (the Johnston Center, in particular) and Antioch University. Huge thanks to the teachers who beamed their light across the very path I wanted to walk—Alexandra Pierce, Kevin O'Neill, Ralph Angel, Barney Childs, Bill McDonald, Frank Blume, Dora van Vranken, Julia Felker, Jo Dierdorff, Jill Ciment, Tara Ison, Alma Luz Villanueva, Diane Lefer, Eloise Klein Healy. You have all left indelible impressions. Thanks to Denise Taylor for reminding me to ask myself whether I know I am standing. Infinite thanks, of course, to Carolyn Sweers, for putting that life-changing strawberry on my desk.

Thanks to the Virgin of the Watermelon for acting as my muse.

Thanks to my agent, Arielle Eckstut. I look forward to continuing our fun and fruitful collaboration.

This book would not have come to full ripeness if it weren't for Renee Sedliar, my brilliant, talented, utterly amazing editor. Working with her has been the greatest gift. Big, big, love to you, sweet Renee.

Everyone at HarperSanFrancisco has been an absolute dream to work with. Thanks, all of you, for believing in me and my work with such enthusiasm. Special thanks to Liz Perle, Lisa Zuniga, Joan Olson, Priscilla Stuckey, and the wondrous Calla Devlin.

Thanks, too, to you, holding this book now. I am so honored to share this path with you—this lush path, this curved path, this scary, joyful, true path. It does my heart good to know there are so many women digging deep into themselves, deep into the rich pulp of language. Write on, fruitflesh goddesses!

Many thanks are due to the following authors and publishers for allowing me to use their fine words in my book:

Diane Ackerman, excerpts from *A Natural History of the Senses* (Vintage, 1990). Reprinted by permission of Random House, Inc.

Virginia Hamilton Adair, from *Ants on the Melon* by Virginia Hamilton Adair. Copyright © 1996 by Virginia Hamilton Adair. Reprinted by permission of Random House, Inc.

Opal Palmer Adisa, excerpt from "Working in My Garden: The Aesthetic Nature of Therapy," by permission of the author.

Margaret Atwood, excerpt from "Bad News," from *Good Bones and Simple Murders*, by permission of Doubleday, "Late August," from *Circe/Mud Poems*. Reprinted in *Selected Poems 1965–1975* by Margaret Atwood. Copyright © 1976 by Margaret Atwood. Reprinted by permission of Houghton Mifflin Company. All rights reserved.

Elizabeth Austen, "Learning Courage," by permission of the author.

Coleman Barks, translation of Lalla. Copyright © by Coleman Barks, *Naked Song* (Maypop, 1992).

Aimee Bender, excerpt from "The Bowl," *The Girl in the Flammable Skirt*, 1998. Reprinted by permission of Doubleday.

Katherine G. Bond, "Wordwalk." Copyright © by Katherine G. Bond, from *The Sudden Drown of Knowing* (Brass Weight Press, 2000). Reprinted by permission of the author.

Rita Mae Brown, excerpt from "Dancing the Shout to the True Gospel . . . ," by permission of the author.

Yvonne Cannon, excerpt from "Into 'The Garden,'" by permission of the author. Originally appeared in *ZYZZYVA*.

Lorna Dee Cervantes, "Summer Ends Too Soon," by permission of the author.

Joan Chase, excerpt from *During the Reign of the Queeen of Persia* (Harper & Row, 1983). Copyright © 1983 by Joan L. S. Chase. Reprinted by permission of HarperCollins Publishers, Inc.

Helen Chasin, "The Word *Plum*," from *Coming Close* (New Haven, CT: Yale University Press, 1968). Reprinted by permission of the publisher.

Robert Fitzgerald, excerpt from *Homer: The Odyssey,* translated by Robert Fitzgerald. Copyright © 1961, 1963 by Robert Fitzgerald. Copyright renewed 1989 by Benedict R. C. Fitzgerald, on behalf of the Fitzgerald children. Reprinted by permission of Farrar, Straus and Giroux, LLC.

Kathleen Fraser, excerpt from "Because You Aren't Here to Be What I Can't Think Of," *New Shoes* (Harper & Row, 1978). Copyright © 1978 by Kathleen Fraser. Used by permission of Marian Reiner for the author.

Robert Frost, from "After Apple Picking," from *The Poetry of Robert Frost,* edited by Edward Connery Lathem. Copyright © 1969 by Henry Holt & Co., LLC. Reprinted by permission of Henry Holt & Co., LLC.

Cristina Garcia, excerpts from *The Agüero Sisters,* by permission of Alfred A. Knopf, a division of Random House, Inc.

Jody Gladding, "Tasteless Melon," by permission of the author. Originally appeared in *Chicago Review.*

Louise Glück, excerpt from "Mock Orange," *First Four Books of Poems,* 1996. Copyright © 1968, 1971, 1972, 1973, 1974, 1975, 1976, 1977, 1978, 1979, 1980, 1985, 1995 by Louise Glück. Reprinted by permission of HarperCollins Publishers, Inc.

Myla Goldberg, excerpts from *Bee Season* (2000), by permission of Doubleday.

Rachel Hadas, excerpt from "Pomegranate Variations," from the collection *Indelible* by Rachel Hadas, Wesleyan University Press. Copyright © by Rachel Hadas. Used by permission.

Sam Hamill, excerpt from Lu Chi, *Lu Chi's Wen Fu: The Art of Writing,* translated by Sam Hamill, 1991, by permission of Milkweed Editions.

Joanne Hayhurst, excerpt from "What Daphne Said," by permission of the author.

Roberta Hill, excerpt from "Immersed in Words," by permission of the author. Originally appeared in *Speaking for the Generations: Native Writers on Writing,* edited by Simon J. Ortiz (Tuscon: University of Arizona Press, 1998).

Jane Hirshfield, copyright © by Jane Hirshfield, from "Great Powers Once Raged Through Your Body," in *Given Sugar, Given Salt* (HarperCollins, 2001). First appeared in *The New England Review,* Spring, 2000. Used by permission.

Ho Xuan Huong, "The Jackfruit," translated by Nguyen Ngoc Bich, by permission of the translator.

Demetria Martinez, "Crossing," from *Three Times a Woman: Chicana Poetry* by Alicia Gaspar de Alba, Maria Herera-Sobek, and Demetria Martinez (Tempe: Arizona State University, Bilingual Press/Editorial Bilingüe, 1989). Reprinted by permission of the publisher.

Carole Maso, excerpt from *The American Woman in the Chinese Hat*, by permission of Dalkey Archive Press.

Lin Max, excerpt from "Stone Fruit," by permission of the author. Originally published in *Calyx* 13, no. 1.

Judy Michaels, excerpt from "On the Sour Sop Tree in Elizabeth Bishop's Yard, Key West" by Judy Michaels, from *Forest of Wild Hands*, 2001. Reprinted with the permission of the University Press of Florida.

Susan Mitchell, excerpt from "Havana Birth," *Rapture* (HarperPerennial, 1992). Copyright © 1992 by Susan Mitchell. Reprinted by permission of HarperCollins Publishers, Inc.

Lorrie Moore, excerpts from *Birds of America* and *Like Life*, by permission of Alfred A. Knopf, a division of Random House, Inc.

Marianne Moore, excerpt from "Nevertheless." Reprinted with the permission of Scribner, a division of Simon & Schuster, from *The Collected Poems of Marianne Moore*. Copyright © 1944 by Marianne Moore. Copyright renewed © 1972 by Marianne Moore.

Linda Lancione Moyer, excerpt from "Listen," by permission of the author.

Ilze Mueller, "Night Shift at the Fruit Cannery," by permission of the author.

Iris Murdoch, from *A Fairly Honorable Defeat* by Iris Murdoch. Copyright © 1970 by Irene Alice Murdoch. Used by permission of Viking Penguin, a division of Penguin Putnam Inc.

Taslima Nasrin, excerpt from "Eve O Eve," from *The Game in Reverse* (George Braziller, 1995), translated by Carolyne Wright and Mohammad Nurul Huda. Reprinted by permission of Carolyne Wright.

Faye Myenne Ng, excerpt from *Bone*, 1993, by permission of Hyperion.

Naomi Shihab Nye, excerpt from "My Father and the Fig Tree," by permission of the author. Originally appeared in *Words Under the Words: Selected Poems* (Portland: Far Corner Books, 1995).

Jenny Offill, excerpt from *Last Things* by Jenny Offill. Copyright © 1999 by Jenny Offill. Reprinted by permission of Farrar, Straus and Giroux, LLC.

Sharon Olds, "Liddy's Orange," from *The Gold Cell* by Sharon Olds. Copyright © 1987 by Sharon Olds. Used by permission of Alfred A. Knopf, a